MW00605227

The at home Gourmet

Everyday *Kosher* Gourmet Cooking for the Home Chef

SARAH M. LASRY

ISRAEL
BOOKSHOP

Copyright © 2010

ISBN 978-1-60091-128-6

All rights reserved.
No part of this book may be reproduced or
transmitted in any form or by any means
(electronic, photocopying, recording or
otherwise) without prior permission of the
copyright holder or the distributor.

Written by: Sarah Lasry
Photography by: Joshua Shaub
Food styling by: Margalit Lankry
Design and Layout: Park Marketing Group /
Rachel Reiner · Esther Silverstein

Edited by:
Hedy Kleinhendler – Peleisrael.com
Sara Goldstein · Rena Hazan
Joahana Palameri

Published by:
Israel Book Shop Publications
501 Prospect Street
Lakewood, NJ 08701

Phone: 732.901.3009
Fax: 732.901.4012
www.israelbookshoppublications.com

Printed in Canada

For My Husband, Dov

Personal Update

I can't believe I am writing another introduction to a new cookbook. I wanted to thank all those people who have supported me, who have come to my cooking classes, book signings and who have emailed me their questions and tips. From Philadelphia, Baltimore, Cedarhurst, Teaneck, Chicago and more, all the way to Israel and Australia, I have been truly blessed to meet and hear from some remarkable loving people. Thank you all - a lot of your suggestions and comments have made their way into this new book.

In *The Dairy Gourmet* I shared with you my ideas, recipes and personal journey of how I opened my little café - Tastebuds. I gave you tips and insights on how I love to create foods that are really a twist on old classics, and use only the freshest ingredients and spices. I talked about my family's influence on how I cook fast and simple and brought to you their best recipes that helped me create my store's famous menu.

Well, it has been a few years since I wrote my last cookbook introduction and, wow, how life has changed drastically for me since then. First, I got married, to a funny generous man named Dov, who has been essential in bringing this cookbook to life. He comes from a small close-knit family where family night dinners consisted of schnitzel and rice or if company was coming, roast with potatoes - a drastic difference from my "French Moroccan" taste buds. As tasty as my mother-in law's recipes are, cumin, curry & tumeric were never words in Dov's vocabulary, let alone something that he was going to eat every day.

Having a husband to come home to and take care of has made me grow as a cook. I have learnt that not everybody has an eclectic palate like I do, that sometimes simple food is best kept simple (with only a hint of a twist) and that when you want to introduce new flavors it has to be exciting, so that the ones who are eating the food are salivating, before they even taste it. I also learned that it's okay to have someone else in the kitchen looking over your shoulder, because sometimes the best ideas for a recipe come from those who are going to essentially eat them. Dov has been, in all honesty and with the tenderest of endearments, the best "guinea pig" a girl could ever ask for. As I know, every home-cook out there can say that about their loving families, who are always willing enough to try every concoction put in front of them.

In this cookbook, I try to give you many recipes that run the gamut; from my mother's every Friday night Chicken Soup with matzo balls to one of my personal favorites, Fried Egg Spaghetti, and healthy meals like Salad Pizza that are quick and easy and don't feel like diet foods. I tried my best to make sure all the ingredients in every recipe are typical things that an everyday cook has in their pantry and fridge. I also want you, the "at home" cook, to explore new foods and expand your cooking repertoire and try new things that will have your family excited to sit down and eat a meal together.

I find that there is nothing more rewarding than friends and family sitting at my kitchen table enjoying something I've cooked. With a hectic schedule and crazy hours I admittedly don't cook every day, and I refuse to feel guilty about that, because I know that sometimes a cold leftover sandwich can be just as tasty and delicious as a gourmet supper. With this cookbook I want to spread the word about making things that are savory and scrumptious that can be great as leftovers the next day and that don't take hours from what precious little time we have. Yet I also want to give you great new ideas about exploring your family's taste buds and taking bold cooking risks that can become your new classic lunch or dinner fare.

Now with the second greatest change in my life, the birth of Fortuna Bracha (Tunie), my beautiful daughter, cooking is going to be even more adventurous and I can't wait to share the fun with all of you in the future. For all you home-cooks out there, whether you're cooking for one or many, new to cooking or a seasoned pro, I hope you find this book a great new addition to your everyday life menu.

Happy Cooking,

Sarah L.

Basics for Every Home Cook's Pantry

Spices: (these are dried)
Cumin
Curry
Tarragon
Tumeric
Rosemary
Thyme
Vanilla Bean
Garlic
Chili Pepper
Crushed Red Pepper
Kosher Salt
Basil
Oregano
Bay leaves
Cream Of Tartar

Jamaican All-spice
Nutmeg
Ginger
Paprika
Cilantro
Parsley
Black & White Pepper

Condiments:
Extra Virgin Olive Oil
Vegetable Oil
White Wine Distilled Vinegar
Balsamic Vinegar
Red Wine Vinegar
Cooking Wine (White and Red)
Mayo

Coconut Milk or Cream
Non-Dairy Whip Topping
Unsalted Butter or Margarine
Creamy Peanut Butter
Tomato Sauce
Crushed Tomatoes
Tomato Paste
Lemon Juice
Brown Sugar
Soy Sauce
Teriyaki Sauce
Ketchup
Apricot Jam
Good boxed Vegetable
or Chicken Broth

Sarah's Essential Home Tips

Here are some great tips that I have collected throughout the years from people, magazines, and other cookbooks that I find to be essential in my every day cooking.

Deglazing a Pan

After sautéing or roasting, look at the bottom of the pan. Those dark food particles stuck to the bottom are caramelized drippings from meat juices. These drippings are loaded with flavor and can be used to make gravy or added to sauces. The best way to capture these flavorful bits is by deglazing. Add any liquid like wine, stock, broth or water to the pan and start scraping vigorously while bringing the liquid to a boil. This is your foundation for any sauce or gravy.

Melting Chocolate

To melt any type of chocolates for dipping or recipes, use a double boiler set over barely simmering water. Take the chocolate off the heat before all lumps are totally gone; they will melt as the chocolate sits. You can also microwave on high power, but stir the chocolate every 30 seconds to keep it from burning.

Dry Herbs vs. Fresh

Dried herbs lack the moisture of fresh herbs; their flavor is more concentrated. However, the majority of the time they will do the same job that fresh herbs will do. Because in the kosher world we are very concerned about bugs, dried herbs are sometimes the only alternative. Therefore, if a recipe calls for 1 tablespoon of fresh thyme, use 1 teaspoon instead. In addition, when cooking with fresh herbs, it's best to add them to the end of a recipe. The heat doesn't destroy their bright color and flavor.

Getting the Cookies You Desire

By adjusting the ingredients you can change the texture of any cookie recipe. If you want: **Chewy cookies** – add melted butter; **Thin, candy-like cookies** – add more sugar; **Cakey cookies** – add more eggs.

Getting the Most of Your Recipe

• Before you start any baking or cooking, read the recipe from start to finish. This makes you familiar with the basic idea of what the recipe requires from tools to ingredients and there are no surprises as you go along.

• One of the main reasons why all the baking and cooking shows look so easy is because all their ingredients are prepped and waiting for them neatly to be used. For most home cooks with little time, though, prepping things beforehand in little bowls is just not realistic. What you can do, though, before actually starting to cook or bake, is to gather all the necessary ingredients and equipment and have them out at the ready. This eliminates the need for you to run around the kitchen searching and lets you focus on the recipe at hand.

• Once you have read the recipe do all the manual labor first. By doing all the required cutting, chopping and dicing at one time you are not only saving time it also makes the recipe easier to follow without breaking the flow to cut or dice something.

• Listen to your recipe. If your recipe ingredient list contains words such as "diced", "sift", "thoroughly stir", or "till golden brown" the author of the recipe is giving you little tips and sensors on how to prepare each ingredient and the dish overall. These tips are invaluable if you want to determine "doneness" on a pastry, create a fluffy cake batter or make an intricate entrée.

• Watch for how the ingredients list is written. A well written recipe has all the ingredients listed in the order that you will need them throughout the recipe. Be careful for those recipe pitfalls. What you may not realize is that the placement of the ingredient description is as important as the description itself. For example: **1 cup rice, cooked / 1 cup cooked rice**
The first way is telling you to take 1 cup of raw rice and cook it; the end result will be much more than 1 cup of rice, as rice expands as it cooks. The second way is calling for 1 cup of rice that has already been cooked; it will stay 1 cup of cooked rice throughout the recipe. The difference between the two ways, about 2 full cups of rice, can make a significant difference in the outcome of your recipe.

• A great recipe is one that is clear and detailed on all aspects of that dish. If you listen to a great recipe at least one time and accomplish it, you now know how to make a flavorful tasting dish that you love and have tried and can then tweak to make in a different delicious way.

Book Hints

Here are some of the symbols you might find in this cookbook, and what they mean:

Found on the top right-hand of photo pages, the "M" and "D" symbols indicate whether the recipe is **Meat** or **Dairy** respectively. If no letter is present, the recipe is pareve.

Mostly found at the bottom of recipe pages, this is just a helpful tip regarding that particular recipe, or ingredients found in it.

BONUS RECIPE
Found below some recipes, this will be an additional recipe relating to the main one on the page.

▸ **Did you know?**
Fun trivia associated with the recipe of the page.

Table of Contents

Amazing Appetizers

Mustard Ginger BBQ Wings

Late one night when I was in my eighth month of pregnancy, my husband and I saw a piece about an all night restaurant that just serves chicken wings and waffles. I can't even describe the cravings that report elicited, so much so, that I made my poor husband go out and beg our local chicken take out place to stay open 10 minutes longer to satisfy my hunger. I am no longer pregnant, but I still have cravings for these chicken wings.

For the Marinade:
12-16 chicken wings, rinsed and patted dry
¼ cup orange juice
¼ cup honey
¼ cup spicy Dijon mustard
¼ cup hickory BBQ sauce (favorite brand)

For the Mustard Glaze:
¾ cup mayonnaise
¼ cup sweet teriyaki sauce
3 tbsp. spicy Dijon mustard
1 tsp. ground ginger powder
1 tsp. garlic powder
1 tsp. soy sauce
Extra ginger powder for sprinkling

Preheat oven to 400 degrees.

Place the chicken wings in a heavy duty Ziploc bag. Mix all the remaining ingredients in a small bowl blending well. Pour mixture into Ziploc bag and gently shake, coating all the wings as best as you can. Place into refrigerator and let marinate for at least 30 minutes or ideally up to four hours or more.

In another small bowl, mix together all the glaze ingredients combining well. Set aside.

Drain and remove wings from marinade and pat dry with paper towel. Place the wings in a large baking tray. Sprinkle ginger powder over the top of the wings, then using a pastry brush coat each wing thoroughly with the glaze mixture that you made. Place into oven and bake for about 20-25 minutes. Remove and pile up onto a plate and dig in.

BONUS RECIPE ▶ **Pareve Ranch Dipping Sauce**

¼ cup mayonnaise
1 cup Tofutti non-dairy sour cream
½ teaspoon dried chives
½ teaspoon dried parsley
½ teaspoon dried dill weed
¼ teaspoon garlic powder
¼ teaspoon onion powder
⅛ teaspoon salt
⅛ teaspoon ground black pepper

Mix together all the ingredients in a small bowl, blending well.
Cover and refrigerate for 30 minutes before serving.

Mustard Ginger BBQ wings

Wild Mushroom Risotto

I have watched many a cooking show and competition in my days, and it always seems like risotto is the hardest thing to cook and to cook well. I never knew what risotto was, so finally one day, I decided to try it. Now, I make it all the time and really don't find it all that hard; in fact, I find it quite easy and versatile.

NOTE: This past December, I cooked recipes that were being judged for a Manischewitz cook-off contest. One of the winning recipes was a risotto that called for Manischewitz borscht. All the judges including myself were very surprised; it was really very delicious and "top five recipes" worthy. For that recipe go to Manischewitz.com and try it!

1 tbsp. extra virgin olive oil
2 tbsp. butter
½ large white onion, diced finely
1 ½ cups sliced Button mushrooms, chopped into small pieces
2 large Portabella or ½ cup Shiitake mushrooms, chopped into very small pieces
1 tsp. thyme
2 cups Arborio rice
1 cup dry red wine
1 quart vegetable broth or pareve chicken stock or broth
½ **cup** grated Parmesan cheese

Have broth ready at a low simmer in a covered saucepan before beginning to make your risotto.

In a large aluminum skillet, on med-high heat, add the olive oil and butter. When butter has almost melted, add the onions and sauté for 3 minutes. Add the mushroom and thyme and mix well; cover pan for a few minutes and allow the mushrooms to cook down and brown (about 3-4 minutes).

Uncover pan and add the rice. Mix everything well with a wooden spoon. Toast the rice in the pan for about one minute. Heat the wine in the microwave for about 30 seconds and then add to the rice in the pan. Mix and let the rice cook for about 2-3 minutes or until the wine has been almost totally absorbed by the rice.

Next, using a ladle, add approximately ½- ¾ cup of the warm vegetable broth; let the rice cook and absorb. Repeat at least 2 more times. Then, decreasing the amount to ½-¼ cup toward the end of the cooking process, add the rest of the vegetable broth. Adding too much broth at the end can result in over-cooked risotto. Run your wooden spoon across the bottom of the pot to determine when each addition of broth is almost completely absorbed.

When the rice reaches a creamy, slightly al dente texture, remove from pan and add the Parmesan cheese. Mix well and let rest for about 2 minutes. Serve warm.

TIP

▸ It is important to add hot stock, not cold, to the rice during the cooking process. Adding cold broth to hot rice results in a hard, uncooked kernel in the center of the grain.

▸ When cooking with broth, if you have used up the broth before the rice is fully cooked, continue with simmering water.

▸ To keep pareve or non-dairy, use margarine and leave out the Parmesan cheese; add a little Kosher salt for taste at the end. You can substitute mushrooms with spinach or butternut squash. Cook those first, set aside and only add to the risotto at the very end of the cooking process.

No Boil Spinach Lasagna

SERVES 6-8

This is really a quick dinner lasagna that I usually make before a fast and reheat the leftovers for the meal after the fast.

2 tbsp. butter
2 cups frozen spinach,
already thawed and drained well
1 tbsp. Kosher salt
1 tbsp. fresh crushed garlic
1 ½ - 2 cups heavy cream
¼ tsp. ground black pepper
½ cup grated Parmesan cheese

16 oz. Ricotta cheese
(or whole milk cottage cheese)
1 large egg
¼ tsp. salt
1 box no boil lasagna noodles
2 cups shredded Mozzarella cheese
(to add a little kick, use 1 cup shredded white
Cheddar cheese and 1 cup Mozzarella)
Extra grated Parmesan for sprinkling

Preheat oven to 425 degrees.

Spinach Alfredo Sauce: In a large sauce pan over medium heat, melt the butter until it starts to foam. Add the spinach, salt and garlic, and sauté for about 3 minutes or until spinach has turned a vibrant green color. Slowly add the heavy cream to the spinach mixture and bring to a simmer, mixing occasionally so the spinach does not stick to the bottom of the pan. When the cream starts to show signs of bubbling, add the Parmesan and pepper. Mix well and let the cream come to a boil. When the cream starts to boil, lower flame and let simmer for another minute or so; remove from flame and set aside.

The spinach alfredo sauce should be thick and creamy in its consistency; add more Parmesan to achieve greater thickness.

Blend Ricotta cheese, egg, and salt in a food processor or by hand until very smooth. In a 9x13 lasagna pan that has been sprayed with non-stick spray, position about 3-4 noodles at bottom of the pan. Using a rubber spatula, spread some of the Ricotta cheese mixture over the noodles; layer 3-4 more noodles and then pour some of the spinach alfredo over those noodles. Sprinkle shredded Mozzarella generously over the spinach alfredo and then layer more noodles. Repeat this process and finish your last layer with the spinach alfredo sprinkled with Mozzarella. Sprinkle a generous amount of Parmesan cheese over the Mozzarella topping. Spray a piece of tin foil lightly with non-stick spray and cover the lasagna. Bake for about 20 minutes. Uncover the lasagna and bake another 10 minutes or until top layer is brown and bubbly.

Cool slightly before cutting into lasagna.

> ▸ If you do not have heavy cream you can substitute with whole milk with a ¼ cup of unbleached flour to make a white sauce.
>
> ▸ Soak your noodles in hot tap water for about 5 minutes; this will dramatically reduce the baking time for your no-boil noodles.

Meat Rollatini with Super Quick Homemade Tomato Sauce

SERVES 6-8

One Sukkoth, quite a number of years ago, I convinced my aunt, Rochie, to let me be in charge of one meal from beginning to end. Now this doesn't sound like such a big deal, but believe me, for my aunt, who doesn't let anyone in her kitchen, and for my uncle Howie and my cousins, who are the world's pickiest eaters, it was a very scary proposition. This recipe was my appetizer, and both my aunt and friends who were there for lunch loved it. My uncle and cousins, on the other hand, managed a few bites before declaring, "Not too bad." From them, it was high praise.

NOTE: This is a great recipe to make on Pesach as well.

1 large eggplant
1 large onion, diced
Extra virgin olive oil
2 tsp. fresh crushed garlic
1 tsp. cumin
1 tsp. oregano
1 tsp. basil
1 tsp. thyme
½ lb. ground beef
(I use lamb sometimes)
½ lb. ground turkey
Kosher salt
Pinch of black pepper

For the Tomato Sauce:
2 tbsp. extra virgin olive oil
½ cup diced onion
2 tsp. fresh crushed garlic
1 tsp. curry powder
2 cups canned, crushed tomatoes
¼ cup fresh chopped basil
1 bay leaf
Kosher salt and pepper to taste
1 tsp. sugar (or 1 packet Splenda)

TIP

I make this rollatini in a breaded version as well. Dredge each piece of eggplant in egg, flour and then bread crumbs (as you would a schnitzel). Pan fry in a little oil and let cool before stuffing with meat. On occasion, I also add vegetables like mushrooms and peppers to the ground meat for a different twist.

Trim eggplant. Cut lengthwise into slices about ½ inch thick. Transfer to a colander and sprinkle lightly with coarse salt. Let stand for about 10-15 minutes.

Heat oven to 375 degrees.

Wipe salt and exuded liquid off eggplant and rub on both sides with 4 tablespoons of the olive oil. Lay eggplants flat on baking sheet and bake until completely tender, turning once. Set aside.

In a large frying pan over med-high heat, sauté the onions in about 2-3 tablespoons of olive oil. When the onions begin to wilt, add the garlic, cumin, oregano, basil and thyme and mix well. Sauté for another few minutes until the onions are soft, and then add the ground beef and turkey to the onions. With the flat part of the wooden spoon, start mixing and breaking the meat into little chunks, while incorporating the onions and spices into mixture. Cover the pan for about 3 minutes and let cook. Uncover, and again with the wooden spoon break the meat chunks into small pieces; sauté for another minute and remove from flame and let cool.

While the meat is cooling, prepare the tomato sauce. In a small sauce pan on med-high heat, sauté the onions in the olive oil. Add the garlic and curry to the onions and mix well. Sauté the onions for another 3-4 minutes or until they have softened and then add the crushed tomatoes. Bring the tomatoes to a simmer and then add the basil, bay leaf, salt and pepper and mix well; bring back to a low simmer. Remove from flame and mix in the sugar.

Assemble the rollatini: Take the cooled eggplant and lay flat on work space. Using a spoon, place a nice heaping dollop of meat mixture in the center of the eggplant. Fold or roll the eggplant over the meat mixture and then place seam side down onto a sprayed 9 x 13 baking dish. Repeat with remainder of the meat and eggplant.

When all the rollatinis have been assembled, pour the tomato sauce generously over top, place into hot oven and bake for 15-20 minutes. Serve hot.

Fried Meat Ravioli

Ravioli can be made a hundred different ways and I am slowly working my way through each possible recipe, it seems. Whenever I need a quick appetizer or side dish I go to the trusty ravioli; fried, boiled, dairy, vegetable, or meat — the possibilities are endless.

For the Ravioli Dough:
3 cups flour
½ tsp. salt
2 eggs
¼ cup vegetable oil
½ cup water
Extra flour on hand for "dusting"

In a mixing bowl, crack eggs and beat with a fork. Add water, oil and salt. Mix together. Add 1 cup of flour to wet mix and stir with fork until it's well mixed. Repeat with the rest of the flour.

Clear and clean off a large surface and dust it with flour. This is where all of your ingredients should be and where you are going to roll out your dough. Take the dough out of the mixing bowl and place on counter. Ball up dough and knead until the dough is pliant. Dust a rolling pin with flour and roll out dough so it is about 1/8 inch thick. Use the top of a glass or a cookie cutter to cut out circles in the dough.

Ball up the rest of the dough and repeat until you have the amount you need. If you have extra dough left, wrap it in plastic wrap and place in the freezer for another time (dough can keep for about a week or so in the freezer).

For the Meat Filling:
1 lb. chopped beef or turkey
2 tbsp. extra virgin olive oil
½ Vidalia onion, diced
1 tsp. fresh garlic, minced
1 tsp. cumin
1 tsp. oregano

1 tsp. basil
1 tsp. parsley
1 tsp. dried chives
½ cup ketchup
2 tsp. Kosher salt
Pinch of black pepper

In a large skillet sweat the onion in olive oil for about 3 minutes. Add the garlic, cumin, oregano, basil, parsley and chives to the onions and mix well. Sauté for another 2 minutes or so. Add the chopped meat to the onions. Using the flat end of a wooden spoon, break up the chopped meat until you get pea-size pieces, while you are also combining it with the onion-spice mixture. Let the meat cook for about 5 minutes, stirring frequently.

After 5 minutes add the ketchup, salt and pepper and mix well. Cover the pan and let the meat cook for another 4-5 minutes. Remove and let cool.

Place a tablespoon of it in the middle of the dough circle. Fill small cup or bowl with water, dip finger in the water and moisten top half of the dough circle. Fold dough circle in half, making sure all filling stays inside and pinch/seal circles to make a half moon shape. Place 1/2 cup of flour in a mound on the counter. Roll ravioli in the flour. Press firmly all the way around the lip of the ravioli with a fork. This will add a "homemade" touch as well as to make sure the ravioli is sealed.

Once all your ravioli is filled, heat a large skillet with 3-4 tbsp. vegetable oil. When oil is hot, gently add one ravioli at a time to pan and fry for about 2 minutes on each side or until golden brown. Make sure not to crowd the raviolis in the pan. Remove with slotted spoon and place onto paper towels. Serve hot with tomato sauce.

Orange Roasted Carrots
with Honey Glaze

SERVES 4

Growing up, the carrot was about the only vegetable I would eat without giving my mother a hard time. It was the perfect food, crunchy and sweet, and you can have contests eating them. My sister Miriam and I did; the first one to nibble all around the carrot and leave the cleanest core would win bragging rights (at least for the hour). I also really love tzimmes, especially the kind my grandmother Meme Malka makes almost every holiday. This is a more sophisticated version that can be served as an appetizer or side dish.

1 ½ lbs. baby carrots or Dutch carrots, scrubbed, with stem on
2 tbsp. extra virgin olive oil
1 ½ tsp. finely grated orange peel
½ cup fresh orange juice
½ tsp. salt
Pepper to taste
1 ½ tbsp. honey

In a large plastic bag add the carrots, olive oil, orange peel and orange juice. Seal the bag tightly and toss until carrots are fully coated. Place bag in fridge for about ½ hour (or overnight) and let carrots marinate.

Preheat oven to 450 degrees. Line a cookie sheet with aluminum foil. Place carrots in single layer on cookie sheet. Pour the remaining juices from bag over carrots. Sprinkle salt and pepper over carrots and cover tightly with aluminum foil. Roast until carrots are slightly tender to the touch (about 10 minutes). Remove foil and drizzle the honey over the carrots. Continue roasting uncovered until carrots are tender and slightly brown in spots (about another 10 minutes). Remove and place carrots and any juices on a platter. Drizzle a little olive oil and a sprinkle of salt and serve hot.

▸ Look for baby carrots that are firm with no brown spots for the sweetest results.

▸ A lot of grocery stores carry miniature versions of vegetables such as carrots, zucchini and squash – that's what you should be looking for. Regular carrots or bagged baby carrots may be substituted.

TIP

Homemade Onion Rings

I love, no, LOVE, homemade onion rings. Actually, I just eat the crust and leave the onions over, but the crust is only good because of the onions inside! Whenever I would go out for a steak, the true test of the restaurant was whether or not homemade onion rings was on the menu; unfortunately, I was let down too many times. Finally, I decided why not enjoy these crispy treats whenever I wanted to? I came up with this very easy and delicious, tangy batter recipe, and now I only have myself to blame for the extra room I need in my skirts.

2-3 large Vidalia onions, cut into ¼ inch round rings
1 ¼ cups flour
⅓ cup cornstarch
1 tbsp. baking powder
1 tsp. Kosher salt
1 tsp. curry powder
1 tsp. oregano
1 ¼ cups ice cold water
Vegetable oil for frying

Heat up a large skillet or small pot of vegetable oil.

In a large mixing bowl whisk the flour, cornstarch, baking powder, salt, curry and oregano together well. Add the ice water to the flour mixture and whisk together creating a slightly watery, lumpy and bubbly batter.

Using tongs or a fork, dip each onion ring separately into the batter, coating it completely, and lightly shaking off any excess drippy batter. Gently place into hot oil and fry. The onion rings are ready when they are slightly puffy and golden brown. Place on paper towels to drain oil and serve hot with ketchup or your favorite dressing.

BONUS RECIPE ▶ **Tangy Dijon Dressing**

Who says you can't have a low-fat dressing with a deep-fried dish? Here is a quick and easy dressing that is delicious with these onion rings.

½ cup plain non-fat yogurt
6 tbsp. sweet pickle relish
2 tbsp. dijon mustard
2 tbsp. whole grain mustard

In a small bowl, whisk everything together and serve.

▸ For a crispier onion ring: right before frying, soak the onion slices in cold water filled with ice for about 10 minutes. Pat them dry before dipping them in the batter.

▸ I use this batter in Tastebuds and at home to fry sliced sweet potato sticks, zucchini sticks, and frozen cauliflower for a vegetable tempura medley.

TIP

Asian Pot Stickers
with Spicy Peanut Teriyaki Dipping Sauce
MAKES 3 DOZEN

Dov and I spent our honeymoon in Israel visiting with family and indulging for a few glorious days at the most amazing kosher Yaarot Ha'Carmel Spa in Haifa. Not only were we pampered luxuriously with spa treatments, but the spa also had some of the most heavenly foods that I have ever eaten. For dinner, there was an embarrassing abundance of menu choices and steamed pot-stickers soon became my obsession. I think Dov and I were the only couple that left the health spa heavier than when we arrived. This is my version of pot stickers that I frequently prepare at the store and at home.

2 ½ tbsp. extra virgin olive oil
½ tsp. curry powder
½ tsp. cumin
½ tsp. ginger powder
½ tsp. dried cilantro (optional)
1 cup shredded green cabbage
1/3 cup chopped leeks
2 scallions
½ cup shredded carrots
1 cup sliced Button mushrooms
2 large Portabella mushrooms, cut into strips
1 red pepper, chopped

2 tsp. soy sauce
1 tsp. Kosher salt
2 cloves crushed garlic
36 wonton wrappers (1 package)*
2 tbsp. cornstarch
Canola or vegetable oil for frying

For Dipping Sauce:
¾ cup teriyaki sauce
¼ cup creamy peanut butter
1 tsp. crushed garlic
Pinch of crushed red pepper (optional)

* I use the Nosoya brand

To prepare the pot stickers: On med-high flame, heat up the olive oil in a large skillet. Add the curry powder, cumin, ginger and cilantro to the oil and mix well; add the cabbage. Coat the cabbage well with the spicy oil mixture, lower heat to medium and cover pan. Let the cabbage cook down for about 3 minutes then add the leeks and scallions. Mix well and sauté everything in pan for another 3 minutes or until leeks turns slightly limp and translucent. Remove from flame and let pan start to cool down.

In a food processor (or by hand), pulse or chop together the carrots, red pepper and both mushrooms two-four times or until coarsely chopped. Add the mixture to the cooked cabbage and mix well. Working with one wonton wrapper at a time, spoon about two teaspoons into the center of each wrapper. Moisten edges of the wrapper with a little water; bring all the edges together into center and pinch points together to seal (it should look almost like a little purse). Place pot stickers on a large baking sheet sprinkled with cornstarch.

In a small pot or a large skillet, heat up about ¼ cup to a ½ cup of oil for frying. The oil should come about ¾ ways up the pot stickers; they should not be submerged fully in oil when frying. Working in batches of not more than 7 or 8 at a time, add the pot stickers to the hot oil and fry until bottoms are a golden brown. Use tongs to rotate pot stickers and brown the tops. Remove and place on paper towels. Repeat process with remainder of pot stickers.

To prepare dipping sauce: In a small pot on med-high flame, add the teriyaki sauce and bring to a simmer. Add the peanut butter to the hot teriyaki sauce and whisk well until the peanut butter is totally dissolved into the teriyaki. Add the garlic and crushed red pepper, mix and remove from flame. Serve the pot stickers hot with a slightly cooled down dipping sauce.

TIP

For the healthier version that was served at the spa, heat 1 ½ tsp. canola oil in a large nonstick skillet over med-high heat. Add no more than 10 pot stickers to pan; cook about 2 minutes until bottoms have turned golden brown. Gently add ½ cup water to pan, cover and cook for about 3-4 minutes. Uncover and cook for another 2-3 minutes or until water evaporates.

This is a great recipe for Yom Tov that can be used as an appetizer. You can prepare and freeze the pot-stickers in advance and store them on wax paper sprinkled with a little cornstarch, so as to keep them from sticking. On Yom Tov, you just fry them in hot oil as needed.

My Favorite Skinny Combo Fries
with Leeks
SERVES 4-6

I first discovered a variation of these Combo Fries with Leeks at Max & David's in Philadelphia, PA, but have since noticed them in quite a few establishments. They are my idea of comfort food. There are days when I run home and make these fries with a nice juicy steak or hamburger, so I can just nosh the night away. They make a great BBQ party side dish.

4 large sweet potatoes, cut into ¼ inch skinny fry
3 large yellow potatoes cut, into ¼ inch skinny fry
1 leek, cut into thin slivers
Vegetable Oil for frying
Kosher Salt
2 tsp. garlic powder
2 tsp. dried basil or oregano
2 tsp. onion powder

Fill a deep heavy pot about 2/3 full of oil and heat to about 350-370 degrees. Lower flame and, working in small batches, fry the potatoes and then the leeks till they turn a nice golden brown.

Place everything in a large bowl and sprinkle well with Kosher salt, garlic powder, basil, and onion powder. Mix well and serve piping hot with your favorite ketchup or mustard.

TIP

For crispy fries, keep cut-up potatoes in ice cold water till ready for frying. Shake them off well and pat dry with paper towel before placing them gently in the hot oil.

Indian Style Spicy Vegetable Samosas

My obsession with Indian food all started on my honeymoon trip with Dov to Israel. One day, while we were exploring the Machane Yehuda Shuk, and I was showing Dov all the unbelievable spices and foods that were in that market, we came across a little kosher Indian vegetarian restaurant hidden amongst the fish and fruit stalls. Daring and under the influence of a very persuasive waiter, we decided to try a little bit of everything, and we had one of the most amazing meals of our lives. To our great disappointment, we couldn't find that same Indian restaurant the last few times we were in Israel although we literally scoured the entire shuk.

3 tbsp. butter
½ tsp. curry powder
1 tsp. cumin
½ tsp. fennel seeds
¼ tsp. turmeric
⅛ tsp. red pepper flakes
Pinch of Kosher salt
1 small onion, diced
1 tsp. ginger
1 tsp. fresh crushed garlic

1 can whole white potatoes, cut into small cubes
½ cup frozen peas
½ cup canned chick peas
½ cup frozen yellow corn
½ cup sliced carrots
Lemon juice
Fresh cilantro
Vegetable oil for frying
24 Wonton wrappers

In a large skillet, on med-high heat, melt the butter. Add the curry, cumin, fennel seeds, turmeric, red pepper flakes and salt and let heat up for about 10 seconds. Add the diced onions to the melted butter and sauté for about 5 minutes or until onions start to wilt. Add the ginger and garlic to onions and mix well. Sauté for another minute or so and then add the potatoes. Mix the potatoes well with the onions and brown for about 3 minutes; add the chickpeas, corn and carrots and mix everything well together. Sauté for about another 2-3 minutes or until the carrots are tender. Remove from heat and let cool down.

Optional: for a more authentic Indian flavor you can add 1 tsp. of lemon juice, and if you desire, 1 tsp. fresh cilantro to the cooled mixture and mix well.

In a large pot, bring your oil to frying temperature. Working with one wonton at a time and a small bowl of water, scoop a spoonful of potato mixture in center of wrapper. Wet the edges of the wrapper and fold into a triangle. Place into hot oil and fry until they turn golden brown. Remove and place on paper towels. Serve hot with coconut dipping sauce.

BONUS RECIPE ▶ Coconut Dipping Sauce

1 can coconut milk   ½ cup creamy peanut butter

Bring coconut milk to a boil; add peanut butter and mix until peanut butter has completely melted and incorporated. Serve warm with hot samosas.

TIP: You can use pre-made ravioli for a thicker, crustier samosa.

Simple Rice Pilaf

Here is a quick, no fail way to make an easy rice side dish that is not pre-packaged. Once you master this recipe, you can add all sorts of other ingredients to make a more substantial, flavorful dish.

NOTE: In Middle Eastern cuisines, many pilafs are flavored with spices, herbs, nuts, dried fruit, chicken, meat or all of the above. Have fun experimenting and creating great new flavors for a simple rice dish.

3 tbsp. extra virgin olive oil or butter
1 ½ cups Basmati rice or long grain white rice
2 ¼ cups water
1 ½ tsp. Kosher salt
Pinch of ground black or white pepper

In a small sauce pan, heat the olive oil over med-high heat. Add the rice to the hot oil and coat well with the olive oil. Let toast for about 3 minutes; remove from heat and set aside.

Bring water to boil in a separate small sauce pan and add the salt and pepper. When the water has come to a boil, pour it over the rice. Bring the rice to a boil and reduce heat to low. Cover and simmer until all liquid is absorbed, 15-18 minutes.

Remove pan from heat, cover with a dish towel, replace lid, and allow rice to sit for about 8-10 minutes. Fluff rice with fork and serve.

BONUS RECIPE ▶ **Portabella Mushroom, Almond & Craisin Rice**

1 small onion diced   *3 large Portabellas diced*   *¼ cup slivered toasted almonds*
¼ cup craisins   *2 tbsp. olive oil*

In a small frying pan saute the olive oil and onions together for about 3 minutes.
Add the mushrooms and saute another 2-3 minutes, add the almonds and craisins.
Cook for another minute and remove from heat. Follow directions to rice pilaf above.
Once rice is made, add the mushroom mixture and mix to combine.

TIP Always rinse your rice well under running water before cooking.

Beer Bread

I am not a baker, especially not of breads; in fact, I think I have a bread baking phobia. It just seems hard and complicated, but I am sincerely envious of my friend Rivky E. who makes baking Artisan breads look as easy as pie. So one day I was searching the web for an easy bread recipe that I might attempt to help me get over my fears and gain some self respect when I came across this easy and terrific recipe. I have only made this recipe twice thus far, but each time it was painless and delicious. Who knows? Challah just might be next!

3 cups unbleached all purpose flour
¼ tsp. instant yeast
1 ½ tsp. salt
¾ cup plus **2 tbsp.** room temperature water
¼ cup plus **2 tbsp.** Budweiser Beer
1 tbsp. white vinegar

1 enameled cast-iron Dutch oven or heavy stock pot

Mix all the dry ingredients together in large bowl. Slowly add the water, beer and vinegar to the dry ingredients and stir gently with rubber spatula. Make sure to scrape up all the flour from bottom of bowl and mix everything well. Cover bowl with plastic wrap or dish towel and set aside at room temperature for about 8 hours.

After 8 hours, shape dough into a ball and knead 10-15 times on lightly floured work space. Place ball of dough in a skillet or shallow bowl lined with parchment paper that has been lightly sprayed or brushed with oil. Spray the top of the dough with non-stick spray, cover with plastic wrap and let rise at room temperature until dough has doubled in size (about 2 hours).

Preheat oven to 500 degrees and place Dutch oven inside to heat up.

Lightly flour top of dough and with a sharp knife, make a long slit along the top of dough. Lower temperature to 425 degrees, and place the dough along with the parchment paper into the heated pot. (Let excess paper hang over pot.) Cover pot and bake for 30 minutes. Remove lid and bake for another 25 minutes or until the loaf is deep brown. Cool to room temperature and serve.

So Cheesy
Onion Potato Gratin

This milchig (dairy) kugel is one of my favorite dishes to make for Shavuoth and really for any time I'm in the mood for warm, cheesy food. This gratin is hearty enough to be a stand-alone supper or to be served as a warm, yummy side dish to a light fish meal.

1 large onion, sliced thin
2 tbsp. extra virgin olive oil
2 lbs. Yukon gold potatoes, sliced into thin rounds
2 ½ cups heavy cream
2 tsp. Kosher salt
Fresh ground black pepper
1 cup grated Mozzarella cheese
1 cup grated Cheddar cheese
1 cup bread crumbs
4 tbsp. melted butter
Extra shredded Cheddar or Mozzarella for sprinkling

Preheat oven to 350 degrees.

In a skillet over med-high heat, sauté the onions in olive oil until they have browned (about 4-5 minutes). In a sprayed 9 x 13 baking pan, layer the bottom with the fried onions. Then layer the potatoes over the onions, covering them completely and overlapping the potatoes one on top of the other.

In a small mixing bowl, whisk the heavy cream, salt, black pepper and both cheeses together. Pour the heavy cream mixture over the potatoes. In a separate bowl, add the bread crumbs and melted margarine, mix well and then spread generously over the top layer of potatoes. Sprinkle with a little more cheese and bake the gratin until it becomes bubbly, the top is brown, and the potatoes are completely soft, about 20-30 minutes. Let gratin rest for about 15 minutes before serving.

BONUS RECIPE ▸ **Vegetable Gratin**

Substitute the potatoes for sliced tomatoes, zucchini and/or eggplant, follow recipe and enjoy!

A few ways to make this slightly more calorie friendly: **1.** Use 1 ½ cups low fat milk with 1 cup heavy cream or cut the heavy cream by half. **2.** Use low-fat or skim Mozzarella cheese only and for added texture and cheesy thickness, some skim Ricotta cheese. **3.** You can leave off the bread crumb topping and just top off with cheese.

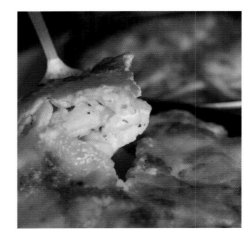

Stuffed Manicotti

I remember like it was yesterday, the first time I ever ate this delicious dish. I was sixteen years old and had just gotten off a plane, sitting in my Aunt Nadia's kitchen in Israel, eating her leftover supper. This dish left such a lasting impression that I have made it a thousand times since.

1 pkg. Manicotti, cooked
3 cups frozen spinach, defrosted & drained
2 tsp. fresh garlic, minced
1 tsp. Kosher salt
½ tsp. black pepper
1 egg
1 pint Ricotta cheese
2 cups Mozzarella cheese
½ cup Parmesan cheese
2-8 oz. cans diced tomatoes
1 tsp. oregano
1 tsp. basil
1 tsp. sugar

Preheat oven to 375 degrees, and grease 9x13 baking dish.

In large mixing bowl mix together the spinach, salt, pepper, and egg. Add the Ricotta cheese, 1 cup Mozzarella cheese, and the Parmesan cheese. Blend well.

Stuff the cooked manicotti noodles with the spinach cheese mixture and lay them in a sprayed aluminum pan.

In a separate mixing bowl combine the diced tomatoes, oregano, basil and sugar. Once combined, pour the tomato mixture over the top of the manicotti. Then sprinkle the rest of the Mozzarella cheese as the final layer over the whole dish. Bake in oven uncovered for 15-20 minutes, or until the cheese has melted and browned slightly.

TIP

Serve one manicotti as a great starter to a dairy meal or serve 3 as a main course with great big lettuce salad and garlic bread.

Cabbage and Meatballs

Of all the yummy things that my Aunt Rochie makes, this is by far my favorite dish. I literally eat the sauce from this dish like it was soup, that's how much I love this dish. It is the lazy man's version of gefilte krout (stuffed cabbage). Now, whenever I need to make a quick and delicious appetizer for Shabbos or Yom Tov, this is always my first choice. This dish freezes beautifully and can be made in very large batches ahead of time.

1 lb. ground beef
½ cup matzo meal
1 egg
1 tsp. Kosher salt
Pinch of pepper
½ tsp. garlic powder

2 bags shredded white cabbage
1 cup ketchup
16 oz. can tomato sauce
⅔ cup brown sugar
2 tbsp. lemon juice
¼ tsp. salt
4 cups water

In a large mixing bowl add your first 6 ingredients; blend together well. This is your meatball mixture. Set aside. Add the rest of your ingredients into a large soup pot and set onto a med-low flame.

While your cabbage sauce is starting to boil, form your meatballs and add to the cabbage sauce mixture. Let meatballs and sauce cook on a medium low flame for about 1 ½ hours. Remove from flame and serve hot over rice, or as is.

Chicken Nuggets

SERVES 4-6

This recipe was taken from my devoted aunt, Rochie, who patiently stands in front of her stove making these fresh practically every holiday that she can.

4 eggs
¾ cup potato starch
¼ tsp. salt
Pinch of pepper
¼ tsp. of basil or oregano
¼ cup vegetable oil

4-6 boneless chicken breasts, cut into small nugget chunks
Vegetable oil for frying

Heat vegetable oil in large frying pan.

In a small bowl, combine the first six ingredients well. Dip chicken pieces into batter and cover chicken well. Using a fork, gently place chicken into hot oil and let fry on each side for about 3 minutes or until golden brown. Remove and drain on paper towel. Serve hot.

BONUS RECIPE ▸ Spicy Corn Dogs

4-5 hot dogs already boiled in water

Make the above batter recipe and add:
1 tsp. curry
1 tsp. cumin
½ tsp. crushed red pepper flakes

Dredge the cooked hot dogs first in flour and then the batter. Fry in hot oil until batter turns golden brown, about 3 minutes.

For fun, stick a chopstick into center of hot dog and serve hot with favorite dipping sauce.

TIP

I use this recipe all the time for almost anything that I want to batter and fry. If I don't have potato starch, I substitute flour and add a little water to loosen the batter as I need.

Corn Dogs

A hotdog on a stick! Battered and deep fried! Oh, how I crave one every time I go to Great Adventures or a carnival. To satisfy this craving, I created my own version that I can make whenever I want. Now if only I could get my own backyard roller coaster…

6-8 hot dogs
3 cups water

1 cup yellow cornmeal
1 cup flour
¼ tsp. salt
⅛ tsp. pepper
¼ cup sugar
4 tsp. baking powder
1 egg
1 cup soy milk

Extra flour for dusting
2 ½ cups vegetable oil for deep frying

Boil water in a large pot. Add hot dogs to the boiling water and let them cook for about 6-8 minutes or until they plump up and start floating to the top. Remove hot dogs, pat dry with a towel, and set aside to cool.

In a large pot heat up the vegetable oil for frying.

In a mixing bowl, combine the cornmeal, flour, salt, pepper, sugar and baking powder, egg and soy milk. Stir it all up until you have a slightly thick batter.

Dust each hot dog well with flour so that your batter will stick. Dredge each hot dog in the corn batter, coating it generously. Place gently into the hot oil and fry for about 2-3 minutes or until the coating turns a golden brown. Remove from hot oil with tongs and place on paper towels to drain off any excess oil. Serve immediately.

If you would like to actually have your dog on a stick, after flouring your hot dog, insert popsicle stick and then dredge in corn mixture.

Simple Soups

Easy Vegetable Broth/Stock

I try to make this stock at least twice a month and freeze it, so I can always have it on hand for any soups or dishes I am making that require it. It takes a little elbow grease with all the vegetable cutting, but it is very easy and well worth the effort.

Stock or broth is used mainly to add layers of flavor to any dish that you are preparing. However, I find that a well spiced dish with the equivalent of water for broth will do the same trick when you don't have broth available.

Happily, as my life gets busier and busier, there has been an increase of really terrific kosher stocks available in stores, my favorites being Imagine brand organic vegetable and no-chicken broths and Manischewitz's new MSG-free and low-sodium chicken and beef broths. I always have a few of these boxes in my cupboard; the one disadvantage is that once you open them they have to be used up right away. I don't recommend refrigerating or freezing them.

However, nothing compares to fresh homemade vegetable stock, and this recipe is truly the best that I have ever made. Don't worry if you are missing an ingredient or two; just increase a different vegetable already being used and the outcome will be just as flavorful.

2 leeks, chopped
1 large onion, chopped
3 celery stalks, chopped
2 carrots, chopped
1 sweet potato, quartered
2 pieces fresh ginger root, chopped
2 parsnips, chopped
1 cup Button mushrooms, whole
1 small tomato, whole
3 bay leaves
Bunch of fresh parsley
Bunch of fresh thyme
1 sprig fresh rosemary
3 tsp. Kosher salt
Fresh ground black pepper
1 tbsp. light soy sauce
15 cups cold water

Place all the ingredients into an extra large stock pot. Bring slowly to a boil and then lower heat and let simmer for 30 minutes at least, stirring from time to time. Cool off, strain and discard the vegetables. The stock is ready to use.

Easy Vegetable Broth/Stock

Split Pea Soup

I must admit I was one of those kids that when it came to peas, I did everything to get out of having to eat them. Thankfully my mother did not make many dishes that incorporated those little green things. When I started Tastebuds, for years I refused to make Split Pea soup because of my pea phobia, until one day a case of split peas by accident was delivered instead of barley. My chef, without my consent, made this soup; my customers loved it and requested it on the menu full time. I finally caved in and tried it, and have become such a huge fan of the pea and this soup, that now I make this meat version at home all the time for dinner.

NOTE: **Pease porridge hot, Pease porridge cold, Pease porridge in the pot nine days old**. This old and very well known nursery rhyme is referring to split pea soup, where in England those who were poor, would make a batch of this soup with whatever meat bones they had and live off of it until the next batch was made.

1 tbsp. extra virgin olive oil
4 pieces of sliced smoked turkey deli or turkey pastrami, cut into small pieces
1 large onion, diced
1 tsp. ginger
2 cloves garlic, minced
1 tsp. cumin
1 tsp. curry
1 bay leaf
1 marrow bone
2 carrots, sliced
1 celery stick, sliced
1 cup yellow split peas
1 ½ cups green split peas
3 cups chicken or beef broth
6 cups water
1 large potato, diced
Kosher salt and black pepper to taste

In a soup pot or small cast-iron oven, stir fry the smoked turkey with olive oil for 4-5 minutes. Add the chopped onions and all the spices and stir well and continue to stir fry for another 3-4 minutes. Add the marrow bone, carrots, celery and both split peas and mix well until everything is well incorporated. Add the broth and water and bring to a boil. When the soup starts to boil add the potatoes and lower the soup to simmer for about 20 minutes. After 20 minutes, remove the bone and bay leaves from the soup with a slotted spoon.

Using a hand blender, blend the soup to a creamy smooth texture, add salt and pepper to taste and then serve hot with crusty bread.

TIP

For the best results, soak both split peas in cold water for an hour. If you don't have deli, a piece of beef stew, chuck or spare rib bone can be substituted. You can leave out the meat as well for a perfect pareve version.

Roasted Cauliflower Soup

Rivky K. once made this soup for her kids for dinner and I loved it. The cauliflower gets roasted in the oven with some salt and olive oil; most times I have to make a double batch because I end up eating half the cauliflower before it ever gets to the soup pot.

3 cups frozen cauliflower florets, defrosted
Extra virgin olive oil
Kosher salt
Black pepper
2 leeks, sliced
1 small onion, diced
1 tsp. thyme
2 tsp. crushed garlic
2 bay leaves
2 carrots, sliced
3 cups vegetable broth
2 cups water
2 large potatoes, diced

Preheat the oven to 400 degrees.

On a large cookie sheet that has been sprayed with non-stick spray, lay out the cauliflower. Generously drizzle olive oil and liberally sprinkle the salt and black pepper all over the cauliflower and lightly toss. Put the cauliflower to roast in the oven for 20-30 minutes or until the cauliflower has browned nicely.

10-15 minutes into the roasting of the cauliflower, you can start sautéing the leeks and onions in the olive oil in the soup pot on med-high heat. After about 3 minutes add the thyme, garlic, bay leaves and carrots and mix well with the onions. Let the carrots tenderize for about 3-4 minutes and then add the vegetable broth and bring to a simmer.

When the cauliflower is ready add it to the soup pot, mix well with the carrots and onions and then add the water and then the potatoes. Cover the soup and cook on the stove top for about 20 minutes more. When the potatoes are soft enough to pierce with a fork, remove the bay leaves with a slotted spoon and use a hand immersion blender to blend the soup to a creamy texture. Use salt and pepper to taste. This soup goes great with garlic croutons or Parmesan cheese garlic bread.

BONUS RECIPE Parmesan Cheese Garlic Bread

Take 1 loaf of crusty French bread and liberally spread it with butter and fresh minced garlic. Sprinkle Parmesan cheese and oregano generously over the bread and bake in oven for 5 minutes, or until bread has toasted nicely.

Mushroom Lamb Soup

This is my go-to Yom Tov Holiday soup. I love to make big batches of it at the start of a two-part Yom Tov like Sukkoth and Pesach. For some reason, I believe this soup gets better and better the later you eat it in the holiday. But because I am a soup lover, this soup rarely sees that second half before it's finished down to the last lamb bone.

NOTE: **Shiitake Mushrooms** – are a larger variety of mushrooms with a cap from two to four inches in diameter and have a brown coloring. The stem is not normally used because of the texture. Shiitake mushrooms have a spongy meaty texture with a bit of a woodsy taste.

Cremini Mushrooms – are similar to Button mushrooms in size and texture. They are light to dark brown in color. The Cremini mushroom is a bit more firm than the Button mushroom and has a more intense meaty and earthy flavoring. The Cremini mushroom is used in the same cooking methods as the Button mushroom and is a good substitute for the Button mushroom for a more intense flavoring.

2 tbsp. extra virgin olive oil
2 leeks, chopped
1 medium onion, chopped
1 cup shredded carrots
2 tsp. cumin
1 tsp. curry
1 tsp. basil
2 tbsp. fresh garlic, minced
1 tsp. dried mint
Kosher salt
Black pepper

4-6 lamb shoulder chops (or stew meat – a cheaper and just as tasty version)
6 cups plus **1 cup** Button mushrooms, sliced
8 large Portabella heads, chopped roughly
½ **cup** sliced Cremini mushrooms
½ **cup** sliced Shiitake mushrooms
2 cups chicken broth (water can be substituted)
2-3 cups water
Salt & pepper to taste

Over med-high heat, using a large soup pot, sauté ¾ of the leeks & onions, as well as the carrots in the extra virgin olive oil. Let the onions cook for about 3 minutes and then add the cumin, curry, basil, garlic, & mint. Mix well, incorporating the spices well with the onions.

While the onions are cooking, salt and pepper both sides of all your lamb chops. Push the onions to one side of the pot and then lay the lamb bones down into the bottom of the pot. Cover the bones with the onions and allow them to pan sear for about 2-3 minutes. Push aside the onions again, flip over the lamb chops, re-cover with the onions and sear on that side for about 2 minutes. After the last 2 minutes remove the bones from pot and set aside.

Add the rest of the leeks and onions to the soup pot. Use a wooden spoon to scrape up all the good bits that are in the bottom of the pot, and mix well with onions. Let the new onions cook for about a minute and then add your mushrooms a cup at a time, mixing well in between each cup. Once all your mushrooms have been added and mixed, place the seared lamb bones back into the pot and add the chicken broth. Cover the pot and let cook for about 25 minutes or until the broth starts to simmer and the mushrooms have softened.

Once the broth is simmering, turn off the flame and temporarily remove the bones with a slotted spoon onto a paper plate. Using a hand immersion blender, puree the mushroom soup.

After the soup has pureed, re-place the soup onto a med-low flame, add the bones, add the additional water and extra sliced mushrooms and cook for about an additional 20-30 minutes. If you desire a thicker soup add less water, or vice versa. Serve hot.

Mommy's Chicken Soup

Until well into the second year of my marriage, I didn't even attempt to make chicken soup for our Friday night Shabbos meal. In my opinion, no one can make it like my mother or, according to my husband, like his mother, who strains the chicken soup so many times until it is this perfectly crystal clear, golden chicken soup. Understandably, I was super intimidated. However, after quite a bit of not-so-subtle hints from my darling Dov, I finally caved in and asked my mother for her soup recipe. I have now become master of the chicken soup (until I go eat at my mother-in-law's).

1 whole chicken cut in quarters with skin removed (4 or 5 pounds)
3 quarts cold water
1 large whole onion
4 carrots, sliced in half
3 stalks celery, sliced in half
1 parsnip
1 parsley root
3 or 4 sprigs of parsley
1 tbsp. of salt
1/8 tsp. pepper

Place chicken quarters in pot with cold water. Cover and bring to a boil. Add vegetables and seasonings. Bring to a boil and lower to a gentle simmer and continue cooking for about 3 hours. Chill overnight and remove fat.

If you are preparing the soup the same day you are serving it, try the following method: After bringing the chicken to a boil, remove from pot and wash under clear running water. Also wash the soup pot in order to remove all the scum. Return chicken to pot, add water and bring to a boil again. Add the vegetables and seasonings and simmer gently. Continue cooking for about three hours. Skim the top of the soup every now and then during the first hour of cooking. When soup is done, taste for seasoning and serve with any one of the following accompaniments: thin egg noodles, matzo balls, soup nuts or boiled rice.

NOTE: For a Sephardic version, strain the soup and discard all the vegetables. Return the soup to the pot and bring to a simmer. Beat two eggs with the juice of ½ a lemon and pour into the simmering soup. Immediately turn off the heat. Stir rapidly to form egg strands. Taste for seasoning and serve.

BONUS RECIPE ▶ **Fluffy Matzo Balls**

4 large eggs
2 tbsp. vegetable oil
½ cup seltzer or club soda
1 cup matzo meal
Salt and pepper to taste

Mix the eggs well with a fork. Add the oil, soda water, matzo meal, and salt and pepper and mix well. Cover with plastic wrap and refrigerate for several hours.

Dip your hands in cold water and make about 12 balls slightly smaller than Ping-Pong balls.

Bring water to a boil in a large pot. Add salt and place the matzo ball in the water. Cover and simmer about 30 minutes or until soft.

TIP

▶ I use chicken from my chicken soup to make chicken salad for Shabbos day. I also love to eat this soup Sunday night; that extra day or so in the fridge makes this soup even more flavorful.

▶ For a darker colored soup with a slightly sweeter taste I sometimes add a whole tomato or sweet potato.

Save time at checkout

Just tap to pay

Your new Chase debit card features contactless technology. Use it for a fast, secure checkout when you see this:

Learn more at chase.com/contactless

Your contactless Chase debit card is easy to use:

FIND
the Contactless Symbol
at checkout.

TAP
your card on
the checkout terminal.

GO
after your payment is
processed in seconds.

Learn more at chase.com/contactless

The Contactless Symbol and Contactless Indicator are trademarks owned by and used with permission of EMVCo, LLC. JPMorgan Chase Bank, N.A. Member FDIC. © 2019 JPMorgan Chase & Co.

New England Corn Chowder

SERVES 4-6

In most restaurants in America this soup/stew is a staple on the menu. It is a hearty soup meal mainly made with some type of fish and best eaten with crusty Artisan bread. It is something that I always wanted to try because of the way I would hear how people rave and salivate about their favorite chowder. This is my version of corn chowder that I usually make at home on those rare snow days that the store is closed and all I want to do is snuggle in my bed with a hot chunky creamy soup and a good book.

2 tbsp. unsweetened butter
5 extra large sticks imitation crab, chopped
4 stalks celery, chopped
1 medium onion, diced
Pinch of Kosher salt
Pinch of black pepper
2 tbsp. flour
1 ear of corn, halved
2 cups of half and half (if not available, you may use **1 cup** heavy cream plus **1 cup** milk)
2 ½ cups vegetable broth
2 medium potatoes, peeled and shredded (about 1 ½-2 cups)
1 can creamed corn
1 cup frozen corn niblets

In an 8-quart stock pot on medium heat, melt the butter. When the butter is melted, add the chopped crab and mix well with a wooden spoon. Let the crab render in the butter for a few minutes and then add the celery, mixing well with the wooden spoon. Let the celery tenderize for a few minutes and then add the onion, salt and pepper. Mix everything well together and let everything cook down for another 3-4 minutes.

Sprinkle the flour over the vegetable crab mixture and mix well, making sure that the flour has fully incorporated and there are no visible signs of lumps. Add the 2 halves of corn to the mixture and then add the half and half and the vegetable broth. Higher the flame to med-high and bring the chowder to a low simmer. When the chowder is at a simmer add the shredded potatoes, and both corns. Mix everything well, and let the soup cook for another 15-20 minutes.

Serve hot in mugs with crusty bread.

TIP

If you don't want to use half and half you can use whole milk or heavy cream. If using whole milk, add flour as needed by the teaspoonful to thicken the soup.

Eggplant & Spinach Creamed Soup

I wanted to make cream of spinach soup one day and totally ran out of spinach. All I had was about ½ a frozen bag full. The only vegetable in my very empty fridge that day was eggplant. What a terrific soup it turned out to be, and this is why I love cooking; you never know when an idea will become a classic.

2 tbsp. extra virgin olive oil
1 extra large eggplant, peeled and diced
1 large onion, diced
½ bag frozen spinach (about 2 cups)
1 tbsp. fresh garlic, minced
4 cups vegetable stock (or water)
½ cup coconut cream (if you do not have on hand, you may use **½ cup** coconut milk plus **¼ cup** sour cream)
½ tsp. nutmeg
Salt and pepper to taste
½ cup light or heavy cream

In a large skillet, heat the oil on med-high heat and add the diced eggplant. Sauté the eggplant for about 3-4 minutes, stirring with a wooden spoon, and then cover the pan. Let the eggplant cook, checking and stirring frequently, making sure not to burn the bottom of the eggplant pieces. Remove eggplant and put into blender and set aside.

In the same skillet add the onions and sauté for about 3-4 minutes. Add olive oil if necessary. Once the onions have begun to wilt and cook down add the frozen spinach and garlic. Cook for an additional 4 minutes.

Remove spinach from heat and add to the eggplant in blender. Pour 2 cups of the vegetable stock, coconut cream, nutmeg, salt and pepper to the mixture and puree until smooth. Pour the eggplant mixture into the small soup pot, add the rest of the stock and bring to a simmer for about 15 minutes.

Once simmering, lower flame and add the cream to the soup. Blend well and heat through, but do not boil. Serve hot garnished with a little Parmesan cheese.

Spicy Beef Ramen Noodle Soup

I once heard about a restaurant in China Town, New York, that serves ramen noodle soup with chopsticks. People stand on line for hours to get a bowl of this ramen noodle soup. What piqued my interest in this particular soup was the undeclared contest that took place in this restaurant during lunch hour. Patrons would vie against each other to see who could continuously eat ramen noodles with their chopsticks without having to remove their chopsticks from the noodles already in their mouth. I just had to make my version of this soup at home to try this!

1 small onion, diced
2 leeks, chopped
2 tbsp. olive oil
2 tsp. fresh minced ginger
2 tsp. fresh minced garlic
1 small package of skirt steak or flank steak, cut into thin strips
1 tsp. cilantro
1 tsp. Kosher salt
Pinch black pepper
Pinch of red pepper flakes
1 large red bell pepper, sliced into strips
1 cup snap peas
2 cups sliced mushrooms (use Button or baby Portabella)
½ cup shredded carrots
1 ¼ tbsp. low-sodium soy sauce
3 cups beef or chicken broth
1 ½ - 2 cups water
1 package ramen noodles
Crispy chow mein noodles

In a soup pot, on med-high heat sauté the onions and leeks in the olive oil for about 3-4 minutes, until leeks have wilted. Add the ginger and garlic to the onions and mix well with a wooden spoon. Place the strips of meat into the pot, mix well with the onions, and then add the cilantro, salt and peppers. Let the meat brown on one side for 2 minutes in the onions and then toss and brown the other side for an additional minute or so.

After meat has browned, lower the flame to medium and scrape the bottom of the pot with the flat edge of your wooden spoon. This will loosen all the flavor bits that have stuck to the bottom of the pot. Add and mix in the pepper, snap peas, mushrooms and carrots to the meat and onions and mix well. Add the soy sauce, combine well and sauté everything for another 4-5 minutes until the vegetables have started to soften. Once the vegetables start to soften add the broth and water and higher the flame to med-high. Let the soup come to a boil and then lower flame and cook for another 5-6 minutes.

Drop in the ramen noodles and allow them to cook in broth for about 2 minutes. Garnish with crispy chow mein noodles and serve hot.

Spicy Beef Ramen Noodle Soup

Cheesy Broccoli Soup

For some reason I always have bags and bags of frozen broccoli in my house. It seems it is the one item I keep on buying at the grocery store because I am always thinking I am out of it at home. So whenever my freezer door no longer closes because of the enormous broccoli bags that are stuffed in there, this is the soup I make.

1 onion, diced
1 leek, diced
2 tbsp. butter
2 cloves fresh garlic, minced
1 tsp. cumin
1 tsp. curry powder
1 tsp. basil
2 tsp. Kosher salt
1 tsp. black pepper
1 ½ lbs. frozen broccoli
2 medium potatoes, cubed
2 ½ cups vegetable broth or water
1 cup whole milk
¾ cup heavy cream
1 lb. shredded Cheddar cheese

In a large soup pot on med-high heat, sauté the onions and leeks in butter for about 2-3 minutes, until soft. Add all the spices and mix well sautéing for another 2 minutes. Add the broccoli and mix it well with the onions and then add the potatoes. Mix everything in the pot well, cover and cook for about 3 minutes and then add the vegetable broth. The broth should cover the vegetables completely; add more water or broth if needed. Cover and cook for about 15-20 minutes, until vegetables are tender.

With a slotted spoon, scoop out about a cup or so of vegetables and set aside. Using a hand-held immersion blender, blend the soup till creamy and then add the vegetables that were set aside, the milk and the heavy cream and mix well. Bring the soup back to a low simmer and add Kosher salt and pepper to taste.

When soup starts to simmer remove from flame and add ¾ of the Cheddar cheese. Mix well until cheese has melted in soup. Serve hot with a nice garnish of more shredded Cheddar cheese.

BONUS RECIPE ▶ Garlic Parmesan Crostinis

1 large French bread, sliced into thin wedges   *3 tbsp. minced garlic*   *2 tsp. oregano*
     1 stick melted butter   *Grated Parmesan cheese*

Preheat oven to 375 degrees. Drizzle olive oil onto a large baking sheet, sprinkle a little oregano and lay out the bread slices side by side. Mix the garlic into the melted butter and drizzle over the bread tops, generously coating them. Then sprinkle bread with Parmesan and more oregano and bake for about 4-5 minutes until lightly browned.

TIP

I recently made this soup for a party that I gave, and it was a huge hit with all my guests. They especially loved it with the garlic Parmesan crostinis that we served with it, for dipping on the side.

Roasted Tomato Soup
with Israeli Couscous

There is nothing like a great tomato soup when I'm feeling blue and tired after a hard day's work to perk me up. I usually take a big bowl of this soup, put on my pj's, cuddle up in bed and call it an early night. It also makes a great, easy, quick supper when you're in a rush and want to serve something hearty.

NOTE: **DO NOT REFRIGERATE** your tomatoes! Cold temperatures ruin tomatoes, hurting their flavor and their texture. You can also cut the acidity of your tomato soup by adding just a teaspoon of granulated sugar at the end of cooking.

For the Roasted Tomatoes:
8 large tomatoes, halved & seeded
2 tbsp. extra virgin olive oil
2 tsp. Kosher salt
1 tsp. black pepper

For the Soup:
2 tbsp. extra virgin olive oil
1 small onion, chopped
1 tsp. cumin
1 tsp. curry powder
3 tsp. minced garlic
Pinch Kosher salt

Pinch black pepper
1 tsp. cilantro (optional)
1 carrot, sliced
1 ½ cups tomato sauce (or juice)
5 cups vegetable stock (or water)
1 cup Israeli couscous

Preheat oven to 375-400 degrees.

On a large baking sheet that has been sprayed with non-stick spray, lay your halved tomatoes face down. Drizzle some olive oil lightly over the tomatoes and sprinkle a little Kosher salt and pepper over them. Place in the oven for about 15-20 minutes.

Remove from oven and set aside to cool. When cooled, chop up the tomatoes into small chunks.

In a large soup pot heat the olive oil and sauté the onions for a few minutes. Add all the spices to the onions and mix them well, making sure the onions are well coated. Sauté for another minute or two. Add the carrots to the onions and mix well; cook gently for about 5 minutes and then add the chopped tomatoes and tomato juice. Bring the soup to a simmer and then add the vegetable stock and the couscous. Bring the soup to a full boil and cook until the couscous is soft and tender (about 20 minutes). Add salt and pepper to taste before serving.

TIP

If you are short on time, substitute the roasted tomatoes with 3 cups of canned diced tomatoes (about 28 oz).

Meatball & Pasta Soup

The general rule of thumb is when you go out on a date, never eat spaghetti or falafel. I once ordered spaghetti and meatballs on a date, and when the sauce and spaghetti began to drizzle down my chin, I realized my faux pas. Lucky for me, my date was away from the table; unfortunately for me, although I was really hungry, I just moved spaghetti around my plate for the rest of the meal. There was no way I would chance a repeat. Although that date was a bust, it reminded me of an Italian wedding soup I had seen in an old cookbook. Hence, my true soup romance!

NOTE: The term "wedding soup" is a mistranslation of the Italian phrase, **minestra maritata** ("married soup"), which is a reference to the fact that green vegetables and meats go well together.

For the Sauce:

1 large onion, diced
1 ½ tsp. cumin
1 tsp. curry powder
2 tsp. fresh basil
2 cloves garlic, minced
½ tsp. ginger
1 tsp. oregano
2 tsp. Kosher salt

Pinch black pepper
2 carrots, sliced
1 stalk celery, sliced
4 cups chicken or
vegetable stock (or water)
2 cans whole roasted tomatoes
½ lb. pasta (small shells or spirals)
1 tbsp. sugar

For the Meatballs:

1 lb. ground meat (I use a combo
of beef and turkey for less fat)
¼ cup bread crumbs (you can use ½ cup
cooked brown rice for a healthier twist)
1 egg
1 tsp. cumin
½ tsp. Jamaican All-spice

½ tsp. curry powder
1 tsp. oregano
1 tsp. parsley
1 tsp. basil
1 tsp. garlic powder
1 tsp. Kosher salt
1 tsp. black pepper

In a large soup pot sauté the onions in olive oil for about 3 minutes. Add all the spices and mix well; sauté for another minute. Add the carrots and celery to the onion mixture and mix well again. Let the carrots and celery cook for about 4-5 minutes, while stirring occasionally, and then add the chicken stock. With your wooden spoon, make sure to scrape the bottom of the pot, mixing the onion mixture with the stock. Add the whole tomatoes, using the wooden spoon or a fork to roughly break up the whole tomatoes into smaller pieces in the soup.

Bring the soup to a low simmer (about 7-8 minutes on medium-low heat) and then add the water (water should make the soup fill the pot about ¾ ways high). While the soup is cooking, make the meatballs.

In a large mixing bowl, combine all the meatball ingredients. Using a spoon or with your gloved hands combine the ingredients and then start to roll small (a little bigger than bite-size) meatballs. Drop the meatballs into the cooking soup, and then the pasta. Cover the soup and let cook on medium heat for about 25-30 minutes. When meatballs are floating to the top and fully cooked, your soup is ready to serve—hot, right off the stove.

Zestful Salads

Health Food Salad
SERVES 6-8

This salad should really be called the Dov Leftover Salad. Dov, my extremely frugal husband, tends to come home with bulk items that he has found on sale. One day it was corn niblets in a can; I think it was "Buy 12 at the price of 6". He brought home 24 cans.

This salad came about when one Shabbos lunch I had a lot of leftover chicken and rice from the Friday night meal, and I really needed to use up the corn that was taking up a lot of space in my pantry. The salad was a big hit and is now made every Shabbos lunch with whatever is left over from Friday night's meat, rice or couscous. This version is the one I make in the store (minus the meat).

For the Salad:
2 Romaine hearts, cut into bite-size pieces
1 package alfalfa sprouts or bean sprouts
1 seedless cucumber, cut into rounds or chunks
1 12oz. can corn niblets
1 cup shredded carrots
2 ripe avocados, diced
2 cups cooked brown rice
¼ cup dried sunflower or pumpkin seeds

For the Dressing:
½ cup mayonnaise
¼ cup teriyaki sauce
2 tbsp. soy sauce
2 tsp. garlic powder
¼ tsp. ginger powder

In a large salad bowl, add all your vegetable ingredients, including the rice and seeds. Mix well.

In a small bowl, add all your dressing ingredients. Blend well with a fork or small whisk until mixture is light brown and creamy smooth.

Add dressing to salad and serve.

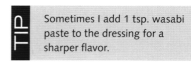

TIP Sometimes I add 1 tsp. wasabi paste to the dressing for a sharper flavor.

Warm Goat Cheese Salad
with Strawberry Vinaigrette
SERVES 4-6

This past Shavuoth holiday I was racking my brains over what I could make that would satisfy a very particular, health-conscious guest whom I wanted to impress. I knew she would not eat anything too cheesy and fattening, but anything too healthy, and my husband wouldn't touch it! You can only imagine my panic over what to do... Hence my brilliant idea (not so much an original one, but I'll take the credit anyway); this delicious warm goat cheese salad. If you have never tried goat cheese, this salad will make you sing its praises to everyone you meet. No matter how many times I have eaten and made this salad, I always close my eyes and savor the sheer delight of that first yummy bite. Now, it is also a great new hit on the Tastebuds Café Menu!

2 7oz. goat cheese log
1 cup bread crumbs (flavored is okay to use)
3 egg whites
2 tbsp. extra virgin olive oil for pan frying

1 head Romaine hearts (washed and chopped into large bite-size peices)
2 cups fresh spinach leaves (washed)
1 cup craisins
1 cup ground walnuts

For the Strawberry Vinaigrette:
½ cup balsamic vinegar
¼ cup strawberry preserves
1 ½ tbsp. extra virgin olive oil (optional; can leave out if you want to keep it a fat-free dressing)

Slice the goat cheese into ½ inch round pieces. Place the bread crumbs and egg whites on separate plates. Take the sliced goat cheese and dip it first into the egg whites and then into the bread crumbs, coating them as you would a chicken cutlet.

Heat up the olive oil in a small sauté pan and gently place the goat cheese into the hot oil. Allow the goat cheese to fry for about a minute on each side until the sides turn crispy, golden brown. Set aside on a paper towel. Work in small batches, adding extra olive oil as needed.

In a separate bowl, add the Romaine lettuce, spinach leaves, crasins and nuts. Mix well. In a separate mixing bowl, add the balsamic vinegar, strawberry preserves and olive oil. Use a whisk and combine thoroughly.

Plate the salad individually with the lettuce mixture. Place about 4 rounds of the warm goat cheese on top of lettuce salad. Drizzle a little of the strawberry vinaigrette on top and serve immediately.

TIP

‣ Fry goat cheese right before serving for creaminess and taste.

‣ You may have heard that Chèvre, French for goat, is cheese made from goat milk. Greek halloumi and Feta cheese are traditionally made from a mixture of sheep's and goat's milk. Until recently, a *chalav Yisrael* version of this cheese did not really exist in our local US grocery stores. I am happy to say it is now readily available. The brand I use is Tnuva (comes in a blue salami-looking package, usually in your yogurt and cream cheese aisle).

Chaya's Salad
(with a twist)
SERVES 4-6

One of my dearest friends, Chaya C., was the first to introduce me to fruit in my salad. Every time I would go to her for Shabbos, she would bring out a version of this salad which I found so appealing that I have shamelessly 'borrowed' her idea. I don't think she even realizes the impact it has made on my culinary repertoire! My one contribution is this awesome garlic sweet dressing that I eat with everything – even sushi!

For the Salad:
2 lb. bag fresh spinach leaves, washed
2 ripe avocados, diced
1 pint cherry or grape tomatoes, halved
2 mangoes, sliced into thin wedges
1 pint fresh blueberries
¼ cup whole or halved walnuts
1 pint fresh strawberries, sliced thin

For the Dressing:
3 fresh garlic cloves, crushed
¼ cup teriyaki sauce
1/3 cup mayonnaise
2 tbsp. apricot jam
1 ½ tsp. white distilled vinegar
Pinch of Kosher salt

In a large salad bowl, combine all your salad ingredients and mix by hand to ensure even distribution of fruit to spinach. In a separate bowl combine the fresh garlic and teriyaki sauce; mix well and let stand for about 5 minutes. Once the teriyaki has been infused with the garlic, add the rest of the dressing ingredients and mix well using a whisk or fork.

Plate salad individually and drizzle liberal amounts of dressing on top.

TIP

▸ If you are serving this salad in a bowl and not individually, leave the spinach out initially and mix the dressing only with the fruits, avocado and nuts. Then add your spinach and hand toss. This way, your spinach will not be too wilted and soggy when it hits your guests' plates.

▸ For this recipe, I like to use the pre-crushed garlic that comes in frozen cubes at your local grocery. This saves a lot of time and is a little more pungent than fresh garlic; 2 to 3 cubes would suffice for this recipe.

Hot Spinach Pesto Salad
with Fresh Tomatoes & Mozzarella
SERVES 4

They say your body craves the foods that give you the vitamins and nutrients that you are sorely lacking. Being borderline anemic (who isn't, really?), I can't seem to eat enough spinach to satisfy my cravings. I especially love spinach hot and creamy, and this is one great way I get my iron fix on a daily basis. I also love eating hot and cold salads combined.

For the Hot Spinach Pesto:
3 tbsp. extra virgin olive oil
2 cups frozen spinach
1 fresh garlic clove
¼ cup pine nuts
2 tbsp. grated Parmesan cheese
Pinch of Kosher salt or sea salt

6-8 plum tomatoes, quartered and then halved into big chunky pieces
¾ cup shredded Mozzarella

Extra olive oil, salt, and pine nuts for drizzle and garnish.

In a small frying pan, heat 2 tbsp. olive oil; add the frozen spinach and garlic and sauté for about 3-5 minutes. In a blender add the cooked spinach, pine nuts, Parmesan cheese, salt and the remaining 1 tbsp. olive oil. Pulse for 1 minute to combine and then set aside.

Plate your tomatoes, sprinkle Mozzarella over the tomatoes and then add the spinach mixture on top. Garnish with a drizzle of olive oil, salt and pine nuts. Serve and enjoy.

TIP

▸ If you're not a huge fan of hot spinach, fresh spinach leaves will also work, or you can use frozen broccoli as another alternative to spinach.

▸ Spinach is considered a rich source of iron and calcium. For example, the United States Department of Agriculture states that a 180 g serving of boiled spinach contains 6.43 mg of iron, whereas one 170 g ground hamburger patty contains at most 4.42 mg.

Watermelon Feta Salad
with Lemon Vinaigrette
SERVES 4

Some people crave only sweets, some only salty things – me, I'm a salty-sweet kind of girl. In the winter, it's popcorn and M&M's, and in the summer, it's this salad! The combination of the sweet watermelon, salty feta and tangy lemon vinaigrette is one of the most refreshing tangy summer salads you will ever have. Makes a great party appetizer, too!

½ seedless watermelon, sliced into bite-size chunks
1 cup Feta cheese, crumbled

For the Lemon Vinaigrette:
¼ cup fresh lemon juice
2 tbsp. olive oil
1 ½ packets of Splenda
Pinch of Kosher salt or sea salt
Fresh mint for garnish

It is best to plate each salad individually rather than mixing it all in a large bowl; the Feta tends to melt when you add liquid.

On each plate, place a generous amount of the bite-size watermelon. Sprinkle chunks of the Feta cheese on top as you desire. In a separate bowl whisk together the lemon juice, olive oil, and Splenda. Drizzle lightly over the watermelon and Feta cheese; top it off with a sprinkle of Kosher salt. Garnish with fresh mint and serve.

TIP

If you do not like to use Splenda, 1 tbsp. of sugar can be substituted instead.

Moroccan Carrot or Beet Salad

SERVES 4-6

For a very long time, I had an unreasonable aversion to beets. I'm not sure if the reason for this is because as a kid you refuse to eat anything that is a vegetable or because it looks yucky, like brussel sprouts or chopped liver, but I really missed out until I was in my teens. It took this salad my Aunt Rochie makes, for me to try beets for the first time. She usually makes both of these versions every Shabbos lunch meal.

6 carrots, sliced into rounds, or
4 whole beets

3 tbsp. lemon juice
2 tbsp. extra virgin olive oil
2 cloves fresh garlic, minced
½ tsp. cumin
½ tsp. paprika
1 tbsp. dried cilantro or ¼ cup chopped fresh cilantro (optional)
Pinch of Kosher salt and black pepper to taste

Bring a medium-size sauce pan full of water to a boil; add the carrots or beets and let boil for about 8 minutes (beets will take 5 minutes longer). Drain and rinse under cold water (after they're cooked, make sure to peel the beets). Cut into bite-size pieces.

In a small bowl, thoroughly combine the lemon juice, olive oil, garlic, cumin, paprika and cilantro. Pour the dressing over the carrots or beets, mix well and serve.

TIP

Cilantro is one of those herbs that people either love or hate. It has a very strong flavor that is a cross between parsley and citrus. It comes from the young coriander plant and is traditionally used in a lot of Middle Eastern, Mexican and Asian cooking. Cilantro is considered an aid to the digestive system. It is an appetite stimulant and is very rich in vitamin C.

Mommy's Shabbos Fruit Salad

SERVES 4-6

Growing up, every Shabbos lunch, my mother usually made a simple fresh fruit salad for dessert. What was so great about this salad was not the actual fruit itself, but the juice that was at the bottom of the salad. My mother also never combined fruits; she kept it either an all citrus, grapefruit and orange salad, or she did a berry version. Both are delicious and caused me and my sister, Miriam, to fight over who would get the leftover liqueur juice at the end!

2 cups fresh strawberries, sliced thin
1 ½ cups fresh blueberries
1 papaya, cubed (optional)

1 cup orange juice
1 tbsp. lemon juice
½ cup orange liqueur
3 tbsp. sugar

In a large bowl, carefully toss together the strawberries, blueberries, papaya, orange juice, lemon juice, orange liqueur and sugar.

Allow them to stand at room temperature for at least fifteen minutes to let the berries macerate with the sugar and liqueur.

> ▸ To make the citrus version of this salad, substitute berries with 3 large ruby red grapefruits and 4 oranges.
>
> ....
>
> ▸ This salad is really great when allowed to macerate with the sugar and the liqueur at least 1-2 hours in advance in the fridge till right before serving. For a really great treat, serve with whipped cream or vanilla ice cream.

Taco Salad
with Sun-Dried Tomato Dressing
SERVES 6-8

I am a huge chip and dip fan. I create dressings that I can slather, so I can satisfy my constant midnight chip cravings. Pathetic I know, but my theory is if you combine vegetables with the chips and dip, it's not really that bad for you. Of course, I tried this in Tastebuds, and it was a huge hit. One day, I decided to change the menu (yet again) and forgot to include this salad. The flak that I got was not to be believed; I had to give in and pay for a costly reprint just so this salad could be included.

For the Salad:
1 head iceberg or 2 Romaine hearts, washed and chopped into bite-size pieces
2 large tomatoes, diced
½ red onion, sliced into thin strips
½ cup sliced black olives
2 ripe avocados, cubed
1 cup shredded Mozzarella cheese
½ cup sharp shredded Cheddar cheese (optional)
2 large handfuls taco chips
1 small mild jalapeño pepper, seeded and diced (optional) for garnish and spice

For the Dressing:
½ cup sun-dried tomatoes, pre-soaked in hot water
2 tbsp. extra virgin olive oil
¼ cup plus **1 tbsp.** mayonnaise
2 garlic cloves, crushed
1 tsp. lemon juice
½ tsp. dried oregano
½ tsp. dried basil
Pinch of Kosher salt

The best way to make this salad is to layer the vegetables instead of mixing them together. Start with the lettuce, and then add the tomatoes, onions, olives, avocado, and both shredded cheeses. Using your hands, crush and sprinkle the taco chips on top of everything. Set aside.

In a blender, add all the ingredients for the sun-dried tomato dressing. Blend well; if mixture seems too thick, add 1 tbsp. at a time of either mayo or olive oil to achieve your desired creaminess. With a spoon, drizzle the dressing over your prepared Taco Salad; garnish with jalapenos and serve.

> ▸ I usually use Golden Fluff brand of tortilla chips. I find that any salty plain corn chips, versus enchilada or spicy chips, work best for this salad.
>
> ▸ I also love to use the sun-dried tomato dressing that I created for this salad for my homemade deli sandwiches. It's a great alternative to the standard ketchup and mustard condiments that we are used to. For an extra kick, add a pinch of crushed red pepper.

Butternut Squash Salad
with Candied Pecans
SERVES 4

Sometime it feels like all I do in my kitchen is cut and peel butternut squash. I use this vegetable so much in my daily life between the Moroccan couscous, soups and ravioli that I make with it, that I secretly think my husband is beginning to resent this particular vegetable. Recently, my obsession with this vegetable has manifested itself into this delicious salad. My poor "over-squashed" husband…

1 ½-2 cups butternut squash cut into small bite-size pieces (½ of a whole squash)
3 tbsp. extra virgin olive oil
1 cup whole pecans
2 tbsp. brown sugar
¼ tsp. cinnamon
Pinch of nutmeg
½ cup orange juice
2 tsp. lemon juice
1 lb Arugula Lettuce or Romaine hearts (or mixed)
2 red Asian pears with peel on & cut into bite-size pieces

In a large frying skillet, over med-high heat, sauté the bite-size pieces of squash in olive oil for about 5 minutes. Lower flame to med-low and cover the skillet; let the squash cook on the flame for another 10-12 minutes while stirring occasionally. The squash is ready when it can be easily pierced with a fork. Remove the cooked squash from pan and set aside.

Using the same frying pan as the squash, scrape up the leftover bits of squash, and leave them in the pan. Add the whole pecans and sauté them over a med-low heat. Add the brown sugar, cinnamon and nutmeg and cook, stirring constantly for about 2 minutes longer. Remove pan from flame and add the pecans to the butternut squash that you set aside.

Again using the same frying pan, stir in the orange juice and the lemon juice, using a spatula to scrape the bottom of the pan. Let the juices come to a simmer and remove from flame.

Place the cut-up lettuce, Asian pears, cooked squash and candied pecans in a large bowl. Drizzle the orange juice mixture over the salad and toss well. Serve and enjoy.

TIP

Did you know that butternut squash is a fruit, that and it originated in Mexico? Tastebud's Mexican Chef, Cosme, is always collecting the seeds of the butternut squash that we use in the store, which he then pan roasts in a little olive oil and Kosher salt on med-low heat for about 10 minutes. Then, for the rest of the day, I see him and the other guys noshing away on handfuls of these delicious seeds.

Dressings

Kickin' Caesar Salad Dressing

There were some complaints about the Caesar salad dressing in my first book The Dairy Gourmet, *so I decided to include another version in this book. I prepare this dressing every day in the store for myself. The only complaint I think that anyone might have now is how addictive this version can become. This Caesar dressing is so good and so simple that you will end up putting it on everything!*

½ cup mayonnaise
1 tbsp. white vinegar
1 package of Splenda or 1 tbsp. sugar
1 tsp. curry powder
1 tsp. garlic powder

Combine all ingredients in small bowl and whisk until creamy.

Ginger Wasabi Mayo Dressing

I sometimes use the liquid that comes in the sushi pickled ginger bottles instead of fresh grated ginger; this will give the dressing a more tangy bite. To substitute the grated ginger, add 2 tbsp. of the pickled ginger juice.

¼ cup mayonnaise
1 tsp. wasabi paste (use less if this is too spicy for your tastebuds)
3 tbsp. sweet teryiaki sauce
2 tsp. fresh grated ginger
1 tsp. garlic minced or **½ tsp.** garlic powder

Pareve Ranch Dressing

1 cup Tofutti sour cream or yogurt
2 tbsp. fresh lemon juice
1 tsp. chopped garlic
2 tbsp. fresh dill, chopped
1 tsp. fresh mint or cilantro
Pinch of Kosher salt
Pinch of black pepper

Mix together all the ingredients in a small bowl, blending well. Cover and refrigerate for 30 minutes before serving.

Homemade Vidalia Onion Dressing

½ **cup** sugar

1 tsp. salt

1 tsp. dry mustard

1 tsp. celery seed

1 large Vidalia onion, grated

¾ **cup** apple cider vinegar

2 tbsp. olive oil

¼ **cup** mayonnaise (optional; can leave out if you want a non-creamy lower-fat dressing)

In a small sauce pan on med-high heat, mix the sugar, salt, mustard seed and celery seed. Add in the grated onions, olive oil and vinegar. Cook until sugar has fully dissolved.

Remove and let cool in refrigerator for 20 minutes. Whisk in mayonnaise for a creamy dressing.

Horseradish Dressing

¼ **cup** mayonnaise

¼ **cup** Tofutti sour cream

1 scallion, thinly sliced

2 tbsp. white horseradish

1 tsp. parsley

Combine in bowl until smooth and creamy.

Jersey Melt
with Homemade Vidalia Onion Dressing
SERVES 2

This was a sandwich that I created way before Tastebuds ever opened. I finally decided to put it on the menu and named it the Jersey Melt; it was and still remains a bestseller.

2 tbsp. extra virgin olive oil
½ red onion, sliced thin
1 red pepper, sliced long and thin
Kosher salt
Black pepper
1 tsp. fresh minced garlic

½ cup shredded Mozzarella cheese or 2 slices Dill Havarati cheese
4 thick slices of country white bread
2 Romaine lettuce leaf
1 small tomato, sliced in rounds
Homemade Vidalia dressing

In a small skillet on med-high heat, add the olive oil. When oil is hot, add the sliced red onions. Let the onions sauté until they have turned translucent and then add the sliced red peppers. Mix well with wooden spoon and add the salt, pepper and garlic. Lower flame to medium, cover pan and let the onions and red pepper cook for about 3-4 more minutes, mixing occasionally. When red peppers have turned medium soft, remove from pan and set aside.

Assemble Melt: Lay 2 slices of bread down; add a piece of lettuce and some tomatoes and drizzle the Vidalia dressing over them. Add the red pepper and onion mixture to the top of the tomatoes; sprinkle generously with cheese, drizzle a little more dressing and top with the other slice of bread. Place on Panini grill or in frying pan that has been sprayed with non-stick spray and pan fry your melt 2-3 minutes each side or until the cheese has started to melt and ooze out of sides. Serve hot with extra dressing.

Homemade Vidalia Onion Dressing:

½ cup sugar
1 tsp. salt
1 tsp. dry mustard
1 tsp. celery seed

1 large Vidalia onion, grated
¾ cup apple cider vinegar
2 tbsp. olive oil
¼ cup mayonnaise (optional; can leave out if you want a non-creamy lower-fat dressing)

In a small sauce pan on med-high heat, mix the sugar, salt, mustard seed and celery seed. Add in the grated onions, olive oil and vinegar. Cook until sugar has fully dissolved.

Remove and let cool in refrigerator for 20 minutes. Whisk in mayonnaise for a creamy dressing.

TIP
▸ You can use any type of bread you prefer.
▸ This Vidalia onion dressing is great reheated and served as a warm dressing for fish or meat.

Jersey Melt

The Ultimate Steak Sandwich

SERVES 2

What's more tasty than a steak sandwich with fried onions and a great dressing? Not much, in my opinion. Because of our weekly BBQ's at home, I always have great leftover steaks at my disposal. However, a great sandwich doesn't have to be designated for leftovers only. I sometimes cook a steak or a small piece of roast, just to make this sandwich.

1 lb. roast
1 ½ tsp. Kosher salt
1 ½ tsp. freshly ground black pepper
1 tsp. freshly ground cumin
1 tsp. vegetable oil
½ Vidalia onion, sliced thin
2 tbsp. extra virgin olive oil
2 club breads

Preheat the oven to 250 degrees.

Combine Kosher salt, black pepper, and cumin in a shallow dish. Roll roast in seasonings, coating well.

Preheat a cast-iron grill pan over high heat. Once the pan is hot, brush the roast with the olive oil, and sear on all sides, approximately 8 minutes total cooking time. Transfer the roast to a plate, cover with aluminum foil, and allow to rest for 10 minutes.

Place the roast back onto the grill pan, put in the oven and cook until it reaches an internal temperature of 135 degrees, approximately 15 minutes. Let roast rest at least 5-8 minutes before slicing. Slice roast to desired thickness and place into club bread. In a large skillet, sweat the onions in the olive oil for about 4-6 minutes. Remove and top your sandwich.

For the Horseradish Dressing:

¼ **cup** mayonnaise
¼ **cup** Tofutti sour cream
1 scallion, thinly sliced
2 tbsp. white horseradish
1 tsp. parsley

Combine in bowl until smooth and creamy.

Garden Fettuccine

SERVES 4

"Pasta, pasta, oh, how I love thee..." Unfortunately, my love affair with all things pasta doesn't seem to be a healthy one. Hence, my quest for lighter versions other than those with heavy cream sauces and cheesy concoctions. Here is one version that I loaded with a ton of vegetables that is super tasty and makes me feel a little less guilty about my pasta obsession.

1 lb. cooked fettuccini (use whole wheat for healthier results)
2 tbsp. extra virgin olive oil
1 small eggplant, peeled and diced
2 heaping tsp. fresh garlic, minced
1 tsp. oregano
1 tsp. basil
1 tsp. Kosher salt
Pinch black pepper
1 cup chopped zucchini
1 red onion, diced
1 cup chopped frozen spinach
1 cup diced tomatoes

Spray a large skillet well with non-stick spray and heat 1 tablespoon olive oil over med-high flame.

Add the diced eggplant and sauté for about 4-5 minutes. Cover skillet but check frequently and stir with a wooden spoon.

Add the garlic, oregano, basil, salt and pepper and stir well. Add the zucchini to the eggplant and sauté for another 3 minutes until zucchini starts to soften. Add left over olive oil, onion, spinach and tomatoes to the eggplant mixture, mix well and cover pan and let cook on stove top for another 4-5 minutes. Add the pasta to the vegetables and mix well, let the pasta cook in the vegetables for another minute or two. Sprinkle a little salt and serve hot.

Sesame Chicken Spaghetti
with Vegetables
SERVES 4

This is another quick and easy recipe I make all the time when I want something tasty for dinner, especially after a hectic day. It also makes a great cold lunch the next day.

1 lb. dark chicken cutlets cut into strips
2 tbsp. extra virgin olive oil
1 tsp. ginger powder
1 tsp. garlic powder
3 tbsp. white sesame seeds

2 tbsp. sesame oil
1 tbsp. extra virgin olive oil
½ cup white wine
1 red pepper, diced
1 yellow pepper, diced
1 cup sliced mushrooms
1 cup fresh or frozen peas
1 lb. spaghetti, cooked
Kosher salt & fresh black pepper to taste

Using a pastry brush coat all your chicken strips with olive oil. On a paper plate, mix together the ginger, garlic and sesame seeds and then dredge the chicken strips into the mixture. Coat each strip well with the sesame seeds.

In a large skillet on medium flame heat up both oils and then add the chicken pieces. Allow the chicken pieces to cook for about 3-4 minutes on each side. When the chicken pieces have turned white and browned all over, remove with tongs and set aside.

Using the same still-hot skillet, add the white wine. Use the flat end of a wooden spoon and start to scrape up all the chicken bits that were left over on the bottom of the pan. As the wine starts to boil down, add both the peppers and let them cook in the white wine for about 3 minutes. Add the mushrooms, mix well with the peppers and cook for additional 3-4 minutes. Add the peas, mix well, then add the sesame chicken pieces, cover and cook for 3 more minutes.

Turn off flame, uncover sesame chicken and vegetables and add the spaghetti to the pan. Mix well and serve hot, garnished with extra sesame seeds.

TIP

I am not a huge fan of white chicken meat so I am grateful that my husband always brings home dark chicken cutlets. For this recipe dark or white works well.

Kickin' Curry Alfredo
SERVES 4

Monday nights are my cooking nights. Because Tastebuds is normally closed on Monday nights, it is the one night I could really take the time and experiment. Thankfully, I have a very forgiving and loving audience Mondays in Dov and Sara G. Dov will sometimes be resigned to try some of my more inventive dishes, whereas Sara G. always eats them with a smile. This one made everyone happy one Monday night.

1 lb. Fettuccine, cooked
4 pieces tilapia

1 tsp. butter
1 cup corn niblets
½ red onion, diced
1 tsp. curry powder
1 tsp. fresh garlic, minced
¾ **cup** heavy cream
½ **cup** grated Parmesan cheese
Kosher salt & black pepper to taste

Sprinkle both sides of the tilapia with a little salt and pepper and wrap in aluminum foil. Bake in oven on 400 degrees for about 8-10 minutes. Remove from oven to cool, then shred into bite-size pieces and set aside.

In a large skillet melt the butter on med-high flame. When the butter is fully melted and starts to brown add the corn niblets and toss. Sauté the corn in butter for about 3 minutes and then, add the red onions. Toss well and sauté for another 2-3 minutes and then add the curry and garlic. Mix well into the corn mixture and then add the shredded tilapia. Pour the heavy cream into the hot pan, lower flame, mix well, and let the cream come to a low simmer. When the cream starts to simmer add the Parmesan cheese and mix well. Let the sauce simmer for another minute or so and then add the pasta. Toss everything together, let the pasta cook for 2-3 minutes in the sauce, and then remove and serve. Garnish with extra Parmesan cheese.

▸ **Did you know?** Curry powder is a mixture of spices of widely varying composition based on South Asian Cuisine. Most recipes and producers of curry powder usually include coriander, turmeric, fenugreek, and red pepper in their blends. Depending on the recipe, additional ingredients such as ginger, garlic, asafoetida, fennel seed, caraway, cinnamon clove, mustard seed, green cardamom, nutmeg, long pepper, and black pepper may also be added.

Fried Egg Spaghetti
with Creamy Spinach
SERVES 4

One night, I was watching The Iron Chef, and the secret ingredient was eggs. Among the various egg dishes the Iron Chef prepared was pasta topped with a fried egg. When the judges cut into that creamy yellow yolk, and it oozed over the pasta, it looked so good, I had to recreate and try it as soon as possible. Now that I'm expecting, this dish and the occasional side of Feta is all I crave.

1 lb. spaghetti, cooked and kept hot

2 pieces white bread, crumbled into little pieces
1 tbsp. butter

2 tbsp. extra virgin olive oil
2 garlic cloves, minced
1 cup frozen spinach
¼ **cup** heavy cream
¼ **cup** Ricotta cheese
¼ **cup** Parmesan cheese
½ **tsp.** basil
Kosher salt
Black pepper

1-2 sunny side up eggs per person

In a large skillet over med-high heat, melt the butter. When the butter has melted and is beginning to brown, add the crumbled white bread. Sauté and mix for about 3 minutes until bread has completely soaked up the butter and has browned. Remove from flame, and set aside in separate bowl.

In the same skillet, heat the olive oil over med-high heat and then add the garlic. Sauté the garlic for one minute, being careful the garlic doesn't burn. Add the spinach to the hot garlic and mix well; let spinach cook for about 4-6 minutes or until water has evaporated, and the spinach has turned a nice bright green. Add the cream, Ricotta cheese, Parmesan, basil, salt and pepper to the spinach and bring to a low boil. Remove from flame and pour over the cooked spaghetti. Mix well.

Fry your sunny side ups. Portion out the spaghetti onto each serving plate. Sprinkle generously with some of the bread crumbs, add the fried eggs and enjoy.

To achieve the perfect sunny side up for this dish there are 2 things you need to do:
1. Use a pre-heated (5 minutes on low) non-stick skillet.
2. Make the eggs at the very last minute and don't cook them longer than 2-3 minutes.

Spicy Taco de Carne

SERVES 4

I was a very ambitious newlywed, and I took it upon myself to prepare my husband a healthy, delicious and inventive dinner every night. One of my better dinner creations was this spicy Taco de Carne recipe. My making dinner every night—well, that lasted about three months…

1 medium white onion, chopped
1 clove fresh garlic, chopped
3 tbsp. extra virgin olive oil
½ tsp. cumin
½ tsp. curry powder
Kosher salt (about 2 pinches)
1 tsp. oregano
½ tsp. crushed red pepper

1 tsp. basil
2 lbs. ground chopped meat
    (can use turkey or beef)
1 cup diced tomatoes
1 cup tomato sauce
1 tbsp. sugar
4 hard taco shells

In a deep frying pan over med-high heat, sauté the chopped onions and chopped garlic in the olive oil until the onions become semi-wilted. Add the cumin, curry, Kosher salt, oregano, crushed red pepper and basil to the onion mixture and sauté until the onions become fully wilted.

Once onions are wilted, add the chopped meat and combine. Using a fork or wooden spoon, break the chopped meat into smaller pieces, about the size of peas. Sauté the mixture until meat starts to turn light brown. Add the diced tomatoes, tomato sauce and sugar to the meat mixture, combining thoroughly.

Loosely cover the frying pan, making sure steam can escape, and lower flame to med-low heat. Allow meat mixture to simmer for about 15-20 minutes until meat is fully cooked and sauce has thickened. Stir occasionally. After meat has fully browned and sauce has thickened, remove from flame and prepare to serve.

To serve: Place heaping spoonfuls of your meat mixture into hard taco shells. Top it off, if desired, with some fresh chopped lettuce and tomatoes. This meal goes wonderfully with fresh corn on the cob.

BONUS RECIPE ▶ **Meat Pizzas**

For my engagement party, I served slices of these pizzas with techina sauce on the side. They were a huge hit.

Use the pizza dough recipe on page 160. Roll into 10-inch pie crust and bake for 10 minutes. Add the meat to the baked pizza crust, top off with a little extra tomato sauce and bake for 3 more minutes. Serve hot.

Barbeque Tilapia Nuggets

SERVES 4

Because I own Tastebuds I spend a lot of my time thinking up recipes that are good for a dairy restaurant. One day Rivky K. was telling me about something that her husband ate which sparked this idea for a barbecued sticky nugget that just happened to be made out of fish. The results are not only a great hit at the store, but at home as well. Make them for your kids; they will be fooled into eating fish for once.

4 large pieces flounder or tilapia, cut into bite size nuggets
1 cup herbed bread crumbs
3 tbsp. vegetable oil

1 cup apricot preserves or jelly
½ cup ketchup
1 tsp. fresh garlic, minced
2 tbsp. distilled white vinegar
1 tsp. ground ginger
Pinch of red-chili pepper (optional)

Preheat oven to 350 degrees.

In a large frying pan heat up the vegetable oil. Dredge each piece of slightly dampened fish into the herbed bread crumbs. Lay gently into the hot oil and fry on each side for about 2 minutes. Remove and place into an oven-safe 9x13 baking dish.

In a small mixing bowl, blend together the apricot preserves, ketchup, garlic, vinegar, ginger and chili pepper. Pour the apricot mixture over the semi-fried fish and bake in oven for 15-20 minutes. Serve with white rice and steamed broccoli.

▸ If you want to really make this quick and easy for your kids, use your favorite brand of fish sticks.

....

▸ If you want to avoid frying, go ahead and bake your fish for 10 minutes in a 375 degree oven and then add the sauce and bake for an additional 8-10 minutes.

"Crab" Salad

SERVES 4-6

I'm always reading or hearing about recipes using crab, such as crab salad, crab cakes, crab tartar... the list goes on and on. So, I finally decided to try the fake crab we use in our California rolls in the store to try out some of these recipes. After all, I have it on very good authority from my sushi chef, David, that the imitation crab sticks we use in the rolls taste exactly like real crab. This is a really great salad to serve for a hearty lunch or for a party appetizer.

For the Salad:

1 package imitation crab sticks, roughly chopped
2 stalks celery, finely chopped
4 carrots, shredded
1 red pepper, finely chopped
¼ cup chopped sweet dill pickles (optional)

For the Dressing:

1 cup mayonnaise
2 tbsp. white vinegar
½ squeezed fresh lemon
¼ tsp. Kosher salt
¼ tsp. dried parsley (if you eat fresh parsley, ½ cup chopped)
¼ tsp. dill

Place all your ingredients in a large mixing bowl. Mix with a spoon, making sure to incorporate everything very well.

Serve on large platter with Melba toast and fresh lemon.

BONUS RECIPE ▶ **"Crab" Cakes**

This recipe, with a few minor adjustments, makes a great-tasting crab cake patty.

Just add about ¼ cup extra mayo or 1 egg, form a patty in your hands, coat patty on both sides with bread crumbs and pan fry in a little olive oil for about 3 minutes on each side... results are m-m-m good!

My Favorite Chicken Salad

SERVES 4

There is this great little place that my husband takes me to in his hometown of Philadelphia called Max & David's. They make the most outrageous chicken salad with currants that I absolutely adore and crave. My husband knows that if he "really loves me" he will go 25 minutes out of his way and bring me home this salad! I am too embarrassed to ask the guys behind the counter what the recipe is, so this is my version (minus the currants) of their salad that I make quite regularly at home.

3-4 cups shredded cooked chicken
¼ cup shredded carrots
¼ cup raisins (or currants)
⅓ cup mayonnaise
½ tsp. garlic powder
2 tbsp. Dijon mustard
1 tbsp. teriyaki
¼ tsp. white vinegar
1 head iceberg lettuce, shredded
½ cup cherry or grape tomatoes, halved

In a mixing bowl, combine the chicken, carrots and raisins. In a separate small bowl, whisk together the mayonnaise, garlic powder, mustard, teriyaki and white vinegar. Pour the mayonnaise mixture over the chicken mixture and combine well.

To serve, place the iceberg lettuce on individual plates or in the center of a large platter. Scatter the grape tomatoes around the lettuce. Spoon a nice heaping of chicken salad on the lettuce and enjoy!

▸ I usually make this for Shabbos lunch and use the leftover chicken from the Friday night meal. You can go to your local deli and grab a rotisserie chicken or a few cooked bottoms or even grilled chicken cutlets to make this salad quick and easy!

▸ The currants or raisins give the chicken that yummy sweet and tangy kick that I love. In the summertime, I use fresh blueberries instead.

TIP

Cobb Salad
SERVES 6-8

Traditionally made with cheese, the Cobb salad was invented by Bob Cobb in 1937. Late one night Mr. Cobb, who owned the famous Brown Derby restaurant, and a friend got the midnight munchies. With the rifled ingredients from his restaurant's ice box, the "Cobb" salad was born. So the legend begins…

For the Salad:
1 cup (6 slices) pastrami or salami
1 head iceberg lettuce or 2 heads Romaine lettuce hearts
3 tbsp. fresh chives, chopped
1½ cups (1 package) sliced cherry or grape tomatoes
1 head fennel, chopped
2 cups cooked shredded chicken
1 cup cooked shredded turkey
2 hardboiled eggs
1 avocado, sliced

For the Dressing:
¼ cup red wine vinegar
¼ tsp. sugar
1 tsp. fresh lemon juice
2 tsp. Kosher salt
¾ tsp. black pepper
¾ tsp. Worchester sauce
¼ tsp. Dijon mustard
¾ cup vegetable oil
¼ cup extra virgin olive oil
1 clove garlic minced

In a small frying pan, with a drizzle of olive oil, pan fry the pastrami or salami for about 1-2 minutes on each side. Slice up into thin strips and set aside until ready for salad assembly.

In a large salad bowl combine all your salad ingredients and set aside.

In a small mixing bowl add all your dressing ingredients. Using a whisk or hand-held blender, mix well. Drizzle on top of salad and serve.

TIP
If you would like to cut the oil, add ¼ cup water.

Delicious Dinners

Dov's Ultimate Steak

SERVES 2

A lucky girl am I, married to the King of all BBQ. Dov can make a mean steak; he's methodical about choosing the right cut, marinating them and cooking them to a perfect medium-rare temperature. Dov will make a BBQ warm weather or in a blizzard; nothing can come in between a man and his steak. Our once-a-week home BBQ has taught me a great deal about meat and its complexities.

For the Marinade:
2 steaks, rinsed & patted dry
3 tbsp. steak seasoning mix (mesquite flavoring)
Kosher salt & black pepper
½ cup teriyaki sauce
2 tbsp. honey
1 tsp. ginger
½ cup Hickory BBQ sauce (or your favorite brand)

For the Glaze:
½ cup teriyaki sauce
2 tbsp. honey
1 tsp. ginger
½ cup Hickory BBQ sauce (or your favorite brand)
2 tsp. spicy dijon mustard (optional)

Preheat oven to 400 degrees.

Take a fork and punch small holes into the meat of your steak. Combine the steak seasoning with the Kosher salt & pepper and rub into the top and bottom of your steak. In a small bowl combine all the remaining marinade ingredients, mix well. Put the steaks into a Ziploc bag and then pour in your marinade. Refrigerate for up to 4 hours or at least 30 minutes before grilling.

Heat your grill. Remove steaks from marinade and wipe off excess with paper towels. Grill off both sides of your steak for about 2 minutes each side. While the steaks are grilling combine your glaze ingredients in a small bowl. Remove steaks from grill and place into aluminum pan. Brush both side of steak with your glaze using a pastry brush and finish cooking in the oven till your steaks reach 130 degrees for medium-rare, (about 8-10 more minutes).

TIP

How to choose the best cut of meat: When possible, buy from the butcher's counter, not the pre-packaged section. Look for steaks that have a fine texture and are firm to the touch. You want the color to be a light cherry-red color, not deep red. And by all means stay away from gray meat. Look for a steak that has marbling. It is the thin threads of fat running through the meat that makes it prime and gives it that incredible flavor. If you do buy packaged meat, stay away from any with excessive moisture, tears or that are past their sell-by date.

Coated Tilapia

SERVES 4

This is a great way to enjoy any white fish, especially tilapia. This recipe came about when my husband asked me to make schnitzel for dinner one night. For some reason, I am not a breaded schnitzel fan; the dry white meat, the thick bread crust, all things that I never grew up with. This tilapia was my compromise to the schnitzel dinner, and my husband only sneaks off once every few weeks to our friend, Naftali's, Deli West for his schnitzel fix.

NOTE: Did you know that tilapia is one of the only fish out there that has a mercury level of almost zero? This makes tilapia one of the healthiest fish.

4 pieces tilapia fillets

2 fresh garlic cloves, minced

Kosher salt

Black pepper

2 cups flour

½ tsp. basil

½ tsp. oregano

4 eggs

4 tbsp. extra virgin olive oil

Fresh lemon for garnish

Preheat oven to 425 degrees.

Prepare each tilapia fillet by rubbing the fresh garlic on both sides of the fillet and sprinkling a little salt and pepper on top of each one. Place on plate and set aside.

In a small bowl, add the flour, basil and oregano. Mix well. In a separate bowl, beat the eggs. Add the olive oil to a large skillet that's on medium heat. Take each tilapia fillet separately, and first dip it into the flour mixture, making sure to lightly coat each side. Then dredge it into the egg mixture and then back into the flour mixture, making sure that the tilapia is well coated on both sides with flour. Place gently into the hot oil. Repeat with rest of the tilapia.

Allow the first side of the tilapia to brown for about 3-4 minutes. Flip the tilapia over and allow browning for another 3-4 minutes. The tilapia should have formed a nice brown crust. Place the skillet into the hot oven for another 2-3 minutes to top the cooking process off. Remove and serve hot.

BONUS RECIPE ▶ **Stir Fried Snow Peas with Shiitake Mushrooms**

2 tsp. soy sauce

½ tsp. sesame oil

2 tbsp. water

1 tbsp. olive oil

¾ cup Shiitake mushrooms, sliced thin

1 tbsp. fresh grated ginger

3 ½ cups snow peas, trimmed

Kosher salt

1 tsp. toasted sesame

In a small bowl, add the soy sauce, sesame oil and water. Set aside. Heat a large skillet with the olive oil. Add the Shiitake mushrooms and cook. Let them brown for 1 minute. Add the ginger and stir fry for another 2 minutes. Add the snow peas and another ½ tsp. of oil if needed, and salt. Stir fry 30 seconds and add the soy mixture and cook for another 2 minutes.

Garnish with sesame seeds.

TIP

Tilapia is sold both fresh and frozen at your local supermarket. I have found that having a bag of frozen tilapia in your freezer is a life saver when it comes to on-the-fly dinners.

Salmon de Carlo
SERVES 4

Here is a tweaked version of my Moroccan Fish that appeared in The Dairy Gourmet. *This salmon dish is not spicy and has loads of vegetables. Along with the Jasmine rice, it makes for a complete, hearty meal. You can also use tilapia for the same delicious results.*

4 salmon fillets (6 oz.)
Pinch Kosher salt
Pinch of pepper
Half of a lemon, juiced

2 tbsp. extra virgin olive oil
1 large zucchini, sliced into thin rounds
2 red peppers, julienned very thin
1 small red onion, julienned very thin
1 tsp. oregano
1 tsp. basil
1 clove fresh garlic, minced
1 can crushed tomatoes (15 oz.)
1 tsp. sugar (optional or use Splenda)
Kosher salt and black pepper to taste

Cooked Jasmine rice (according to package directions)

Preheat oven to 375 degrees.

Using a non-stick spray, prepare a 9x13 pan. Lay each salmon flat side down in pan, sprinkle salt and pepper on top of each fillet, then pour the lemon juice over. Cover and bake for 10-15 minutes in oven, or until salmon is nice and pink on the inside.

While salmon is baking, sauté all the vegetables in the olive oil for about 5-6 minutes on med-high heat. Add the oregano, basil, and garlic and mix well; sauté for another 3 minutes while consistently stirring the vegetables with a wooden spoon. Add the crushed tomatoes, sugar, salt and pepper to the sautéed vegetables. Mix well, cover pan and allow vegetables to cook in the tomato sauce on stove top for another 4- 5 minutes. Uncover and lower flame to low; let sauce simmer until salmon is ready.

When salmon has cooked to perfection, plate the rice with salmon on top and generously portion the de Carlo sauce over each salmon fillet. Serve hot.

TIP

When I'm really pressed for time, I don't prepare the sauce separately as above. I just place the raw fish in a 9x13 baking pan, smother it with the raw vegetables and lots of tomato sauce, cover it and let it cook for about 30-40 minutes in a 350 degree oven. The salmon doesn't look as pretty but tastes just as delicious.

One Pot Garlic Herb Chicken & Potatoes

SERVES 4

It's amazing what your body craves when you're pregnant. For me it was coke, Feta cheese and whole cooked garlic. Out of desperation for lots of cooked garlic I came up with this chicken one pot recipe. I just can't explain; why, now that I have my daughter, Tunie, do I still crave whole cooked garlic?

NOTE: For all the green herbs that I use in this recipe, I buy the fresh frozen cubes which I let defrost and can then spread nicely with my fingers over the chicken skin. I also buy whole peeled garlic to make this a fast and easy recipe.

1 whole chicken
2 heads of garlic (about 20 cloves)
1 bag boiler onions, tops cut off
and semi peeled (pearl onions will work as well)
Kosher salt
Fresh ground black pepper
2 tsp. fennel seeds
2 tsp. fresh dill

2 tsp. cilantro
2 tsp. ginger
2 tsp. parsley
extra virgin olive oil
6 Yukon gold potatoes, peeled & quartered
Pinch smoke red paprika (sweet red paprika will do)
1 ½ cups semi dry white wine

Preheat oven to 400 degrees.

On a plastic cutting board stuff the whole chicken with a quarter of the fresh garlic and as many boiler onions as you can fit. Lay the chicken belly up and generously sprinkle salt and pepper onto its skin and in its cavity. Use your hands to massage the salt and pepper into the skin. Do the same with half the fennel seeds and half of all the herbs.

Place the whole chicken into a Dutch oven belly down, and repeat sprinkling the salt and pepper and rubbing the herbs on the top side of the chicken. Drizzle a little olive oil over the top of chicken, lightly glazing.

Add your quartered potatoes around your chicken, and then add the rest of the garlic and onions. Sprinkle with a little paprika. Pour the white wine into the pot so that it comes to a little less than halfway up the chicken. Place pot into oven and let cook covered for about an hour. Remove cover and then cook for another 30-40 minutes, checking periodically and making sure not to burn the bottom of the chicken. If necessary add a little more white wine or check for doneness and remove.

Serve hot with lots of fresh bread to spread the warm cooked garlic.

TIP

When selecting garlic, it should be big, plump and firm, tight silky skins with its paper-like covering intact, not spongy, soft, or shriveled.

1 head or bulb of garlic = approximately 10 to 15 cloves
1 small garlic clove = ½ teaspoon minced garlic = ⅛ teaspoon garlic powder
1 medium garlic clove = 1 teaspoon minced garlic = ¼ teaspoon garlic powder
1 large garlic clove = 2 teaspoons minced garlic = ½ teaspoon garlic powder

▸ **Did you know?** Raw garlic is used by some to treat the symptoms of acne and there is some evidence that it can assist in managing high cholesterol levels. It can even be effective as a natural mosquito repellent.

Baked Chicken Legs
with Colored Peppers
SERVES 4

This dish is a great quick supper or Shabbos meal dish. It's part of my 'prep it and forget it' repertoire of dishes that I love to make.

4 chicken quarters

½ cup favorite brand honey mustard

¾ cup teriyaki sauce

1 tbsp. extra virgin olive oil

1 large Vidalia onion, sliced thin strips

3 yellow peppers, sliced into long strips

3 red peppers, sliced into long strips

¼ cup sesame seeds

½ cup soy sauce

1 clove fresh garlic, minced

1 tsp. sugar

6 whole pieces of fresh garlic cloves (optional)

Preheat oven to 350 degrees.

Lay your chicken quarters skin side up in a large baking pan. In a small bowl, mix the honey mustard and teriyaki together. Pour generously over the chicken, coating them well. Set aside.

In a large skillet, over med-high heat, sauté the onions for about 1 minute. Add all the peppers and the sesame seeds and mix well. Sauté for another minute and then add the soy sauce, garlic and sugar to the peppers; mix very well and cook for another 2-3 minutes. Remove peppers from flame and pour them over the top of the chicken, smothering them completely. Sprinkle in the whole pieces of fresh garlic, cover pan and place in oven.

Bake for about 1½ hours. Uncover and bake for an additional 20-30 minutes or until chicken browns on top. Serve hot.

▸ I love to serve this over Jasmine rice for a main course dish that has a great Asian flair.

▸ If I make this for a Friday night meal, I purposely add 1 or 2 extra peppers to the recipe, and before I serve the dish, I set aside a small amount of peppers. These peppers are super delicious eaten cold, and I add them to my Shabbos leftover salad the next day.

Plum Lamb with Pears
in Red Wine Sauce
SERVES 4

Since I have birch allergy, I cannot eat soft peeled fruit unless it is cooked. All my favorites, like pears and apples, usually end up in some type of chicken or meat dish, so I can still enjoy them. My friend, Rivky E., makes a Mediterranean chicken that I absolutely love. I have tweaked her recipe so many times that I am not sure what the original one is anymore. However, this is my favorite version.

1 tbsp. extra virgin olive oil
4-5 lamb steaks
Kosher salt and pepper
¼ cup honey
2 tsp. fresh mint, chopped fine
2 cups good red wine (choose one that you love to drink)
2 Asian pears, peeled, cored and sliced thin
1 cup whole dried prunes

Heat up the oil in a Dutch oven or a small stock pot on med-high flame. Pat the lamb dry, sprinkle with salt & pepper and then using a pastry brush coat the lamb with the honey. Sprinkle the chopped mint on both sides of the lamb and lay each piece gently into the hot oil. Let the lamb cook and brown, 1 minute on each side and them remove with tongs and set aside.

Lower flame and add the red wine to the hot pot. Use the flat end of a wooden spoon and scrape up the brown bits on the bottom of the pot and mix with the red wine. Then add the sliced pears and whole prunes and cover the pot. Let the pears and prunes cook in the red wine for about 3-4 minutes. Uncover pot and add the lamb back into the pot. Cook for an additional 20-25 minutes. The red wine should have reduced significantly. Remove lamb onto platter, let stand for at least 8 minutes before serving. Spoon the warm plums and pears with wine on top of the lamb and serve.

Herbed Chicken Breast
SERVES 4

Before I was married, I cooked at home for friends and family once in a blue moon. Now a married woman, I cook at home more often. At least once a week I have this dish on the menu. It's filling, so easy and always delicious. Most importantly, my husband really appreciates all the great 'effort' I put in preparing his dinner!

NOTE: For this recipe I use the fresh frozen herb cubes that they sell in your local grocer's freezer section (Bodek or Dorot brand). I let them defrost so I can rub the herbs easily into and on the chicken.

4 chicken thighs

3 tbsp. extra virgin olive oil
4 tsp. dill
4 tsp. parsley
4 tsp. ginger
4 tsp. garlic
4 tsp. cilantro
2 tsp. Kosher salt
1 tsp. fresh black pepper
1 cup white wine

Preheat oven to 375 degrees.

Brush the chicken thighs with olive oil making sure to brush under the skin and in all the crevices. In a small mixing bowl combine all your herbs, making a paste-like mixture. Using a knife or your fingers spread the herb mixture over the tops of the chicken including the underside of the skin.

Place the chicken into a baking dish, and gently pour your wine into the bottom of the pan. Cover the pan and bake in oven for about 40-45 minutes. Uncover and cook another 10-15 minutes or until done.

BONUS RECIPE ▶ Couscous with Sweet Potatoes & Onions

Plain couscous,
made according to directions
2 tbsp. extra virgin olive oil
½ Vidalia onion, diced
1 tsp. cumin
1 tsp. cinnamon

1 tbsp. brown sugar
½ tsp. nutmeg
½ tsp. All-spice
2 large sweet potatoes,
diced into small cubes
Kosher salt to taste

In a large skillet sauté the onions in olive oil on med-high flame. Add the spices and mix well with the onions. Lower flame and add the sweet potatoes and let cook for about 6-8 minutes with skillet covered. Uncover and mix with wooden spoon and cook for another 2 minutes. The sweet potatoes should be soft with a little hard edge to them. Pour over top of hot couscous and serve.

BONUS RECIPE ▶ Red Quinoa with Vegetables

¾ cup red quinoa
1 ½ cups chicken broth
(or stock)
Vegetable oil cooking spray

1 lb. fresh sugar
snap peas, strings removed
1 red bell pepper, cored,
seeded, and thinly sliced
2 tbsp. chopped fresh mint

Cook quinoa until toasted, 3 to 4 minutes. Add broth; bring to a boil. Cover, reduce heat to med-low and simmer until quinoa absorbs liquid, about 20 minutes. Turn off heat; let sit, covered, until ready to serve. Heat 1 tablespoon oil in a large skillet over med-high heat. Cook sugar peas and peppers until crisp-tender, about 3 minutes. Season with salt and pepper. Turn off heat. Add mint and toss. Pour vegetables over quinoa and serve.

TIP

Before I go to work, if I am not running too late, I try to throw the chicken thighs into a Ziploc bag with some lemon juice and sweet white wine for an extra boost of flavor.

Veal Beef Stew

SERVES 4-6

There is really nothing better than a hot stew in the oven for dinner after a hard day's work. That is, until you realize you are the one that has to cook and prep the stew!

Growing up, my mother always made a stew goulash type of dish for dinner that my siblings and I love. As kids it seemed she threw a lot of stuff in a pot, and —ta-da—20 minutes or so later, supper was served and it was delicious. I make stew for dinner quite a bit using whatever meat and vegetables I have in the house. Here is one of my versions of stew that is quick and easy.

1 lb. boneless shoulder meat, cut into cubes	**½ tsp.** black pepper
1 lb. bonless veal shoulder meat, cut into cubes	**2 cups** sliced mushrooms
¼ cup flour	**1** small bag baby carrots
2 tbsp. extra virgin olive oil	**2 stalks** celery, diced
1 large onion, diced	**1** large zucchini, sliced
2 cloves garlic minced	**2 cans** whole potatoes, quartered
1 tsp. cumin	(or 6 Yukon gold potatoes, peeled & quartered)
1 tsp. curry	**1 ½ cups** chicken stock or water
1 tsp. oregano	**½ cup** dry red wine
1 tsp. basil	**¾ cup** Hickory brown sugar BBQ sauce
1 tsp. smoke red paprika (sweet red paprika will do)	(or your favorite BBQ sauce)
2 tsp. Kosher salt	

On a med-high flame, heat up your stew pot. While your pot is getting hot, dredge all your meat cubes in the flour, shaking off the excess and placing them directly into the bottom of the hot stew pot. Let the meat cubes brown on all sides for about 2-3 minutes, remove from pot and set aside.

In the same stew pot, lower flame to medium and add the olive oil. Use a wooden spoon to scrape up all the brown bits in the bottom of the pot and mix with the olive oil. Add the onions and all the spices and sauté for about 4 minutes or until onions have wilted and turned translucent. Add the mushrooms and mix well with onions, cover pot and continue to cook for about 3 minutes.

Add the baby carrots, celery and zucchini mixing well with the mushrooms and onions and cook for another 2 minutes. Replace the beef cubes into the pot; add the potatoes, the chicken stock, red wine and bbq sauce. Mix well, cover pot and cook on stove top for about 20 minutes bringing the stew to a simmer. Uncover and cook for another 4-8 minutes. Serve hot in bowls over rice or couscous.

TIP

▸ I am proud to say, that when time is short and I am tired after a full day's work, I use bagged baby carrots, canned whole potatoes (which are my favorite) and whatever other frozen vegetable I feel would be a great addition to that day's stew. This makes things very quick and super easy and does not skimp.

▸ I like to cut my own cubes of stew meat. However, if you want to save time, most local butchers sell cubed beef stew meat and cubed veal stew packages.

▸ **Did you know?** Goulash – Gulyás in Hungarian, a word meaning "cattle stockmen"– was the stew they would typically eat every day lunch and dinner.

Chicken Pot Pie Pasta

SERVES 4

I am one of those people who buy frozen packages of fresh vegetables, pack them into my basement freezer and forget about them until there is no more room for anything else. Whenever this happens I pull out this recipe and solve my dilemma till the next time. Chicken pot pie is an American staple that is served in practically every home. I took that idea and made a pasta-meat dish with a pareve cream that is now a staple at my home.

1 ½ cups frozen peas
1 cup frozen diced carrots
1 ½ cups frozen corn niblets
2 tbsp. extra virgin olive oil or canola oil
3 tbsp. margarine
1 small onion, chopped
3 stalks celery, chopped
2 cups cubed chicken breast
1 ½ cups chicken broth
¼ cup Tofutti sour cream
¼ cup soy milk
3 tbsp. flour
1 tsp. curry powder
2 tbsp. dried parsley
1 tsp. Kosher salt
1 tsp. black pepper
1 lb. penne or ziti noodles, cooked

Preheat oven to 400 degrees.

Toss frozen vegetables with the olive oil and spread evenly onto a sheet pan. Place into oven and cook for about 6 minutes or until golden brown.

In a small bowl microwave and heat the broth, mixed with the pareve sour cream and soy milk. Set aside.

In a saute pan heat 1 tablespoon of margarine and cook the onions and celery for about 4-5 minutes. Add the chicken pieces and let them cook until they turn white (about 4 minutes). Add 2 more tablespoons of margarine to the celery mix and cook out the water. Add the flour and curry and cook for 1 to 2 minutes. Whisk in the hot broth mixture and cook until thickened. Add the parsley, salt and pepper. Remove from heat and toss in the cooked vegetables, mixing well.

In a large casserole dish filled with the cooked pasta, pour in the vegetable mixture. Bake in the oven for 10-15 minutes or until bubbly. Serve immediately.

TIP To save even more time I will use 2 cups shredded leftover roasted chicken.

Mommy's Asian Chicken & Spaghetti

SERVES 4

I have literally grown up on my mother's Asian Chicken and Spaghetti, and my sister Miriam and I make it quite often for our own families. I like mine super saucy while my sister's dish is quite a bit drier; my very diplomatic nephews, Eliezer and Ephraim, don't discriminate and will down heaping bowls of both. But secretly, I know...

1 box spaghetti
1 lb. skinless chicken cutlets cut into thin strips
1 tbsp. extra virgin olive oil
3 cloves fresh garlic, minced
½ cup soy sauce
3 tbsp. sugar
Pinch of ground ginger

Put the spaghetti up to boil. While the spaghetti is boiling, prepare the chicken.

In a large skillet on med-high flame, heat the olive oil and garlic. Do not let the garlic burn. Add the chicken strips to the hot skillet and cook for about 1 minute. When the chicken starts turning white, add the soy sauce, sugar and ginger. Coat all the chicken pieces well with the sauce and cover pan for about 4 minutes. Occasionally, uncover pan and stir, making sure the chicken is not sticking to pan and the soy sauce is not burning.

When chicken has been fully cooked (try not to overcook), remove from flame and add the hot spaghetti to the chicken and soy sauce mixture. Using tongs, fully coat the spaghetti with the soy and chicken mixture. If it seems too dry, add more soy sauce to the spaghetti mixture and mix well. Serve hot.

Chicken Curry

SERVES 4-6

If you haven't noticed my obsession with all things curry, this dish will make it quite evident. I usually make this dish when I need something filling, and I'm in the mood of something different for dinner. Recently, I served this dish one Friday night, and a seven-year-old guest literally licked her fingers clean. My obsession is slowly spreading...

2 lbs. baby chicken drumsticks (or sliced chicken thighs)
¼ cup of flour
2 tbsp. extra virgin olive oil
1 onion, diced
2 tsp. curry
1 tsp. cumin
1 tsp. Kosher salt
1 tsp. black pepper
1 tsp. cilantro
1 tsp. thyme
1 tsp. basil
2 cups sliced mushrooms
1 cup shredded carrots
1 cup canned chickpeas
½ cup coconut milk or cream
½ cup white wine
½ cup chicken stock

Preheat your cooking pot on med-high flame. Lightly coat your drumsticks in flour and gently place onto bottom of hot pot. Sear your baby drumsticks on all sides for about 3-4 minutes total. Remove drumsticks from pot and set aside.

Use the same pot (without washing it) and sauté the diced onions in olive oil. Gently deglaze the bottom of pot using the flat end of a wooden spoon. Add the spices and mix them well with the onions and let cook for about 3-4 minutes. Add the mushrooms and mix well; cook for 3 minutes and then add the carrots and chickpeas. Add the coconut milk, wine and chicken stock, combine all ingredients well, cover pot and let cook for about 4 minutes more. Add the drumsticks you set aside, lower flame to medium and cook on stove top for an additional 30-40 minutes. At the end of this time your Chicken Curry liquid should be reduced by more than half; if not, uncover pot and let cook for an additional 5 minutes. Serve hot over basmati rice.

Margalit's Moroccan Meatballs

SERVES 6-8

One Friday afternoon on my regular "hide-from-the-world-at-Starbucks-in-Barnes-and-Noble" hour, I met my good friend, Margalit L. I asked her what she was making for Friday night dinner. Since time was running short, and I hadn't yet even entertained the idea of cooking, I thought I could get Divine inspiration or at least an invite from her. Instead, she disclosed this recipe. Although I didn't get the invite that time, I did get the best recipe for Friday night dinner ever! I literally make it all the time. You're the best, Margalit!

5 extra large white onions, sliced into thin strips
3 tbsp. extra virgin olive oil
2 tsp. cumin
1 tsp. curry powder
1 tsp. turmeric
1 tsp. ground Jamaican All-spice
Kosher salt and ground black pepper to taste

For Meatballs:

1 lb. ground lamb
1 lb. ground chicken or beef
1 egg

¼ cup bread crumbs
2 tsp. cumin
1 tsp. Jamaican All-spice
1 tsp. dried chives
1 tsp. dried parsley
1 tsp. Kosher salt
Pinch ground black pepper

2 cups beef broth or (1 cup red wine +
         1 cup water or broth)
¼ cup raisins

Preheat oven to 350 degrees.

In a large Dutch oven or a pot that can be placed in the oven, over med-low flame, heat the olive oil. Add the onions and all the spices to the oil and mix well. Sauté the onions for about 3-5 minutes while stirring frequently. Bring flame to low and cover pot. Mix every minute or two to prevent the onions from sticking to the bottom of pot.

In a large mixing bowl, add the 2 ground meats, egg, bread crumbs, and all the spices. Mix well.

Using a slotted spoon, remove half of the onions from the pot and place into a separate bowl. Shape meatballs into golf ball size and place them gently into the pot, nestling them among the onions. Once all the meatballs are in the pot, cover them with the remaining onions.

Raise the flame to medium-low, add the beef broth or red wine and raisins, cover pot and cook for about 15-20 minutes. After 20 minutes, mix everything gently with a wooden spoon and put into hot oven for 30-45 minutes or until broth has reduced to less than half. Remove from oven and let cool slightly before serving meatballs. Serve meatballs over Jasmine rice.

Crusted Veal Chops
with Spinach and Corn Succotash
SERVES 4

I always serve veal chops for special occasions like birthdays and anniversaries. It has become my personal celebratory meal; so much so, that whenever Dov sees me making them he knows good news is to follow. So now I make them on occasion for dinner, just because. It always brings an instant smile to Dov's face and makes me less predictable.

Crusted Veal Chops:
4 veal chops
Kosher salt & pepper
2 tbsp. extra virgin olive oil
3 tbsp. Dijon mustard
1 cup cornmeal
1 tsp. basil

On a large plate mix together the cornmeal & dried basil.

Pat veal chops dry with paper towels. Sprinkle with salt and pepper. Over high flame, heat oil in heavy, large, ovenproof skillet. Add veal. Cook until brown, about 1-2 minutes per side. Remove from heat.

Using a pastry brush, lightly coat the veal chops with mustard. Then press cornmeal mixture onto top and bottom of veal chops. Roast in oven until cooked to desired doneness, about 15 minutes for medium-rare.

Spinach & Corn Succotash:
2 tbsp. margarine
2 cups canned corn
1 cup frozen spinach
2 tsp. Kosher salt
½ tsp. fresh black pepper

In a large skillet heat up the margarine on a med-high flame. As the margarine melts, add the corn and cook for about 3 minutes. Then add the spinach, salt and pepper and mix well with the corn. Let the spinach and corn cook for about 5-6 more minutes, until spinach is fully cooked and any excess water has evaporated. Serve hot.

▸ **Did you know?** Because of the relatively inexpensive and more readily available ingredients, succotash was popular during the Great Depression in the United States. It was sometimes cooked in a casserole form, often with a light pie crust on top as in a traditional pot pie.

Veggie Bowl
SERVES 2

When I am feeling like I have indulged myself way too much in chocolate and ice cream and my body is screaming for protein and veggies, I eat this dish. It is super filling and chock full of good stuff that is tasty, and best of all, doesn't feel like diet food.

1 8 oz. piece salmon fillet
1 4-6 oz. piece tilapia fillet
Kosher salt & pepper
1 tsp. fresh garlic, minced

1 red onion, sliced
1 cup chopped frozen broccoli florets
1 cup chopped frozen cauliflower florets
2 large Portabella mushrooms, sliced thin
¼ cup teriyaki sauce

Preheat oven to 400 degrees.

Take 2 pieces of aluminum foil. Lay each piece of fish separately in foil. Sprinkle fish with salt & pepper; add a little fresh garlic to both pieces and then fold and close each piece of fish in their respective foil. Place them in oven and let them cook for about 6-8 minutes.

As the fish is cooking, spray a large skillet and place on med-high flame. Add the onions and sauté for about 3 minutes. Add the broccoli and cauliflower and sauté for about 3 minutes and then add the sliced Portabellas. Cover the top of the pan and let the vegetables sweat for 2 more minutes; then add the teriyaki sauce. As the vegetables cook in the teriyaki sauce, take out the 2 pieces of fish from the oven and add them to the vegetables. Break up the fish as you mix them into the teriyaki vegetables. Cook for an additional few minutes until broccoli and cauliflower are tender and ready to eat. Serve as is or over brown rice.

▸ **Did you know?** Protein is a part of every cell in your body, and no other nutrient plays as many different roles in keeping you alive and healthy. Its importance for the growth and repair of your muscles, bones, skin, tendons, ligaments, hair, eyes and other tissues has been established. Without protein, you would lack the enzymes and hormones you need for metabolism, digestion and other important processes.

Turkey Chili

SERVES 4-6

I'm always trying to create one pot recipes that are healthy and hearty, use up the vegetables in my fridge, and make great leftovers for lunch the next day. This Turkey Chili fits that bill perfectly. The ingredient list looks intimidating but includes all things that I usually have in the fridge or sitting in the cupboard, and the leftovers are great in sandwiches and over pasta.

2 tbsp. extra virgin olive oil
1 white onion, minced
1 red pepper, diced
1 yellow pepper, diced
1 zucchini, diced
2 cloves of garlic
1 tbsp. chili powder
1 tbsp. cumin
¼ tsp. ground coriander
½ tsp. red pepper flakes
1 tsp. oregano

3 tsp. Kosher salt
Pinch of black pepper
Pinch of cayenne pepper
2 lbs. lean ground turkey
½ cup canned red kidney beans
½ cup canned corn
1 (14.5 oz.) can diced tomatoes
1 (8 oz.) can tomato sauce
2 cups beef broth

2 cups cooked wild rice

In a large skillet, heat the oil on medium heat. Add the onion, peppers, zucchini, garlic, and all of the spices; let pan cook, stirring often, (about 8-10 minutes). Stir in the ground turkey, breaking up the meat into small pieces with the edge of a wooden spoon. Let the ground turkey cook with the onions for about 3-5 minutes. Stir in the beans, corn, diced tomatoes, tomato sauce and broth and bring to a boil. Cover, lower heat, and simmer while stirring occasionally for about 30 minutes.

Remove cover from turkey chili after 30 minutes and let simmer uncovered for another 5 minutes. Serve the turkey chili hot over the wild rice.

TIP

You can use any type of ground meat for this recipe. Substitute 1 lb. of beef for turkey and serve in a hard taco shell, topped with homemade guacamole for a very tasty chili taco.

Whole Wheat (Diet) Pizza

SERVES 2

When Tastebuds first opened, we sold what we called 'vegetarian wraps'. One day, instead of rolling a vegetable laden wrap, I left it opened and cooked it like a pizza for lunch; it was one of my most successful creations. I calculated the Weight Watchers points, renamed it the Weight Watcher Pizza, and we now sell hundreds of these pizzas a day in the store.

2 12-inch whole wheat tortilla wrap
2 cloves fresh garlic, crushed
½ cup tomato sauce
¼ cup sliced tomatoes
1 cup frozen spinach, thawed and drained
1 cup sliced Button mushrooms
1 red pepper, sliced long
¼ cup black olives
½ cup frozen broccoli
½ red onion sliced
4 oz. low-fat or skim grated Mozzarella cheese
Pinch of dried oregano
Pinch of Kosher salt
Pinch of black pepper

Preheat oven to 375 degrees.

For this recipe you need to evenly divide all the ingredients between the two tortillas.

Spray non-stick spray on a large cookie sheet or baking pan. Lay tortilla flat on tray, and spread the fresh garlic all around. Pour tomato sauce onto tortilla and spread evenly and then start layering each vegetable ending with the onions, one on top of another, like you would when making a traditional vegetable pizza. Top all the vegetables off with grated Mozzarella, sprinkle some oregano, salt and pepper on the pizza and place in hot oven.

Bake pizza for about 15 minutes or until cheese has fully melted and the edges of the tortilla have turned crispy brown.

TIP

In the store, I use 12-inch whole wheat wraps which are about 4 points each. At home though, I usually buy the 6-inch whole wheat or spinach wraps that are about 2.5 – 3 points each and are the perfect size for a light dinner that includes a soup or side salad.

Stuffed Portabella Mushrooms

SERVES 4

I love farmers' markets, vegetable stands, and my local Stop and Shop vegetable aisle. Anything that displays fresh produce, strange as it sounds, really makes me happy. Maybe it's all the bright colors on display or the possibilities of good yummy things to be made that are healthy; I'm not entirely sure. Even though I may have Chocolate Frosted Donuts in my cart, the moment I see the beautiful fresh produce display, I aspire to eat healthy and fill my cart beyond what I will ever really make. As a result, I would often find my fridge full of produce that needed to be used or it would inevitably be trashed. This is how the stuffed Portabella came to be included in my lunch and dinner repertoire.

4 extra large Portabella mushrooms
1 ½ tbsp. extra virgin olive oil
½ red onion, diced
1 ½ cups frozen spinach, defrosted and drained
1 crushed garlic clove
1 ½ tsp. Kosher salt
1 large heirloom tomato, cut into thick round slices
1 ½ cups grated Mozzarella cheese

1 cup home-made marinara sauce or favorite jar marinara sauce

Preheat oven to 400 degrees.

To prepare the mushrooms:
Using a small teaspoon, clean out the inside of each Portabella, removing the black underside and keeping the mushroom whole and intact. Using a damp paper towel, wipe each mushroom to clean any dirt or debris.

Lay out the Portabellas top side down onto a small baking sheet. Make sure to spray your baking sheet with non-stick spray first. With a small pastry brush coat each Portabella with a little olive oil and sprinkle a little Kosher salt on top. Place into oven and let cook for about 10-12 minutes. Remove from oven and set aside.

While Portabellas are cooking, in a small frying pan on med-high heat, sauté the onions in the olive oil until they turn limp and translucent. Add the spinach, garlic and salt and sauté for another 3-4 minutes. When spinach has cooled down slightly and the Portabellas are ready, it is time to assemble.

Assemble by placing a heaping spoonful of spinach into the center of Portabella. Lay one large round slice of tomato on top of spinach mound, sprinkle liberally with Mozzarella cheese. Place stuffed mushrooms in hot oven, and bake for about 5-8 minutes or until the cheese has turned bubbly and golden brown.

Serve hot with marinara sauce.

Zucchini Pancakes
with Feta Cheese

My grandmother, Meme Malka, makes the best potato latkes, hands down. It doesn't have to be Chanukah; she serves them any time, any day, to everyone and anyone who comes to eat at her house. In my childhood, I have spent many occasions in her kitchen, hand-grating potatoes till my knuckles were raw. One day, I decided to make them at home for Dov, but of course why should I have potatoes in my pantry when I need them? So, out came the zucchinis that I had, and then the experimenting began... I must say these are not Meme Malka's potato latkes, but they are a very tasty latke alternative.

2-3 large to medium zucchini, grated coarsely
Kosher salt
Black pepper
1 large egg, beaten
3 scallions, chopped thinly
½ **cup** flour
½ **cup** Feta cheese
4 tbsp. bread crumbs
2 tbsp. fresh dill
⅓ **cup** extra virgin olive oil
Sour cream or Greek yogurt for garnish

In a medium bowl, grate the zucchinis, sprinkle Kosher salt and pepper liberally over them, and mix well. Cover bowl with plastic and let the zucchinis soak for 10 minutes.

Using your hands, squeeze out excess liquid from the zucchini in small batches and transfer to a separate mixing bowl. Once you have transferred all the zucchini, add the egg, scallions, flour, Feta cheese, bread crumbs and fresh dill and mix well with a fork.

In a large frying skillet over med-low heat, heat up the olive oil. Scoop out the zucchini cheese mixture by the heaping tablespoon and drop into the hot oil. Let zucchini latke fry on one side for 2-3 minutes and then flip over and fry again for another 2-3 minutes. Repeat in small batches and serve hot zucchini latkes with a dollop of sour cream or Greek yogurt as garnish.

BONUS RECIPE > Meme Malka's Potato Latkes

This is how she gave me the recipe verbatim.

"For every potato you hand-grate, you add an egg; add some salt and pepper, but make sure you kvetch all the water out of the potatoes very well. Mish it with a fork or sometimes I use a hand blender. Fry it in oil and then eat."

Take it from me, follow these directions exactly, and you will achieve the best-tasting latkes you have ever eaten!

Ratatouille

SERVES 4

I first learned about this dish during my seminary days a long time ago... My fellow classmate Leiba Z.'s cousin lived right by our school, and we would go to her for 'survival' dinners. Leiba's cousin would trade these free 'survival' dinners for free babysitting. Everyone was happy, especially me who loved to come and eat Ratatouille, something I never had before then.

NOTE: What does the word "ratatouille" mean? Ratatouille is a French dish. The name is comprised of two components: "**rata**" is a slang word from the French Army meaning "chunky stew", and "**touiller**" means "to stir". Thus, the meaning of the word is, "a chunky stew that is stirred".

2 tbsp. extra virgin olive oil
2 cloves garlic, crushed and minced
1 large onion, quartered and thinly sliced
1 small eggplant, cubed
1 yellow bell peppers, coarsely chopped
1 red pepper, coarsely chopped
1 can (14.5 oz.) diced tomatoes
1 can (14.5 oz.) whole tomatoes
3 to 4 small zucchini, cut into 1/4-inch slices
1 tsp. dried leaf basil
1 tsp. dried leaf oregano
1 tsp. thyme
2 tbsp. fresh parsley, chopped or **1 tbsp.** dried parsley
½ tbsp. sugar or **½ packet** of Splenda
Kosher salt and pepper to taste

In a Dutch oven or large saucepan, heat olive oil over med-high heat. Add garlic and onions and cook, stirring often, until softened, about 5-6 minutes. Add eggplant; stir until coated well with oil and sauté for another 2-3 minutes. Add peppers; stir to combine. Cover and cook for 10 minutes, stirring often to keep vegetables from sticking to bottom of pan.

Add tomatoes, zucchini, and herbs; mix well and mash down the whole tomatoes into small chunks and mix well with all the other vegetables. Cover and cook over low heat for about 15 minutes, or until eggplant and zucchini are tender. Add the sugar, salt and pepper, mix well and let simmer for another 2 minutes. Remove and serve hot, separately or over rice or pasta.

TIP

This makes a great light lunch or dinner; it can be served as a stand alone meal with rice or as a side dish for fish or meat, or as a great topping on pasta.

Salmon Burgers

My husband, Dov, is a meat eater. Fish is not his thing, so getting him to eat it once a week to control his cholesterol is quite a challenge. In creating this recipe, I found that good quality canned salmon, as opposed to fresh tuna, combined with spinach, held better and produced a juicy, healthy alternative to the traditional beef burger.

½ cup frozen spinach
1 tbsp. extra virgin olive oil
2 cloves fresh garlic, chopped
1 can pink salmon (14 oz.), drained
2 egg whites
¾ cup Italian bread crumbs
1 tsp. dill or parsley
Big pinch of Kosher salt
Big pinch of black pepper
2 tbsp. extra virgin olive oil
Whole grain burger buns
Romaine lettuce
Sliced tomatoes
Sliced red onions

In a small skillet, on med-high heat, sauté the spinach and garlic in olive oil. Allow the spinach to cook for about 3-4 minutes or until it turns soft and bright green. Set aside to cool down.

In a large mixing bowl, add the salmon, egg whites, bread crumbs, dill, salt, and pepper and the cooked spinach. With a spatula, mix everything together well, until all ingredients are fully incorporated. Form the salmon burger patties.

Heat up 2 tablespoons of olive oil in a frying pan; when oil is hot, add the salmon patties one at a time; do not crowd the pan. Allow the patties to cook for about 3-4 minutes on one side; flip over and cover pan and cook patty for additional 3-4 minutes. Remove and plate, placing one fish patty on a burger bun; garnish with lettuce, tomatoes and onions. Serve hot or cold.

BONUS RECIPE ▶ Ginger Wasabi Dressing

Look on page 90. This dressing is a great addition to add to your salmon burger as a garnish. If you prefer to bake your salmon burger in the oven instead of pan fry, to ensure a moister burger, brush this dressing generously on all sides of the burger and then bake for 10-15 minutes in a 350 degree oven.

▶ This is a great healthy meal to serve your kids. If the green of the spinach is too much of a tip-off that there might be vegetables hiding, use chopped up cauliflower instead.

▶ If you are on a no-flour diet, you can substitute the bread crumbs with oats. You can also bake instead of pan-fry your salmon burger.

TIP

Salad Pizza

I find that whenever I cater events, I really get inspired and usually produce some of my most successful recipes. This recipe was created for a baby shower whose guests were all very conscious of their weight. I needed low-caloric hors d'oeuvres and came up with a mini version of Salad Pizza using whole wheat flour and low-fat salad dressing. It was the perfect party bite.

NOTE: This pizza dough recipe makes enough dough for 2 crusts which will freeze beautifully wrapped tightly in plastic wrap for up to 3 months.

Really Easy Pizza Dough:
(makes 2 10-inch thin crust pizzas)

¼ cup warm water
1 1/8 tsp. dry yeast
½ cup water, room temperature
4 tbsp. extra virgin olive oil
2 cups flour
(can use whole wheat or white all purpose)
1 ½ tsp. Kosher salt

For Salad Pizza Topping:
(for 1 pizza)

½ cup grated low fat Mozzarella cheese
1 Romaine heart, chopped
3 tbsp. sliced black olives
3 tbsp. favorite low-fat dressing
(I use the Kickin' Caesar on page 90)
Parmesan cheese for garnish (optional)

Preheat oven to 350 degrees.

In a small bowl, pour in the warm water and then add the yeast (do not mix). Let the yeast stand for about 5 minutes or until it softens. Mix the yeast gently in the water to dissolve, cover bowl with towel, and allow to stand for another 15 minutes. Add the room temperature water and 1 tbsp. of the olive oil to the yeast and mix to combine.

In a mixing bowl with the paddle attachment, add the flour and salt. On low speed, mix the flour slightly. Continue on low speed, adding the yeast water and the rest of the olive oil and slightly increase the speed on the mixer to incorporate (about 2 minutes). Switch to a dough hook attachment and knead dough on medium speed for about 4 minutes until dough turns smooth. Remove dough from bowl onto floured counter and knead by hand for another minute. Place dough into a lightly oiled bowl and cover with plastic wrap. Place in warm spot and let poof for an hour.

When dough has doubled in size, divide into two parts. Using a floured rolling pin and surface, form one part into a ball and roll out into a 10-inch circle; top with grated Mozzarella cheese and place onto a sprayed baking sheet. Bake for 10 -15 minutes.

Assemble your salad in a mixing bowl, placing all the ingredients together and mixing well. When pizza is hot out of the oven, layer the salad on top and then slice and serve hot.

BONUS RECIPE **Eggplant Stromboli**

Cut one small eggplant into ½ inch thick slices, dredge each piece in egg and then breadcrumbs and fry in oil.

Using this pizza dough recipe, divide one ball into 2 pieces. Roll out into three 5-6-inch rounds. Place 2-3 pieces of fried eggplant on center of each pizza; add ¼ cup of tomato sauce and a handful of grated Mozzarella cheese on top of eggplant and then fold one side of the dough over the eggplant creating a half moon shape. Crimp edges firmly together.

Brush the top of Stromboli with olive oil, sprinkle a little Kosher salt and bake for 20 minutes in a 350 degree oven.

TIP
If you have no desire to make your own pizza dough, frozen dough or a piece of your local favorite pizza shop dough will do just great. You can also make the salad with any vegetable and favorite low-fat dressing that you desire.

Whole Wheat Pizza Dough

I am not normally a fan of whole wheat anything, especially pizza. However, due to the ever-changing food trends, whole wheat pasta and pizza is a must-have for any café. I discovered a version of this recipe in one of my old magazines, tweaked it and came up with really delicious dough. I now on occasion make it at home to rave reviews.

1 (¼ ounce) package active dry yeast
1 cup warm water
2 cups whole wheat flour
¼ cup wheat germ
1 tsp. salt
1 tbsp. honey
¼ cup grated Parmesan cheese (optional)
2 tsp. oregano
1 tsp. garlic powder
2 tbsp. extra virgin olive oil

Preheat oven to 350 degrees.

In a small bowl, dissolve yeast in warm water. Let stand until creamy, about 10 minutes.

In a large bowl combine flour, wheat germ and salt. Make a well in the middle and add honey, Parmesan cheese, oregano, garlic powder and yeast mixture. Stir well to combine. Cover and set in a warm place to rise for at least 20 minutes.

Roll dough on a floured pizza pan and poke a few holes in it with a fork. Lightly coat the top and sides of the pizza with the olive oil, using a pastry brush.

Bake in preheated oven for 5 to 10 minutes, or until desired crispiness is achieved.

 Even though this dough is very tasty as is, the longer you let this dough rise the better it becomes. So, if you have time in the morning before work, put up a batch and let it rise a whole day.

Mediterranean Tuna Pita

SERVES 4

I am such a huge ice cream fanatic that before I eat meat I think: do I really want to be fleshig or am I going to want that ice cream later? As pathetic as I admit that to be, it has led me to create some great non-meat dishes like this Mediterranean pita sandwich. If I eat a healthy meal, I deserve and feel way less guilt, when I am eating my delicious ice cream reward!

2 whole wheat pitas, halved
1 can dark tuna
1 green apple, peeled & diced
1 Asian red pear, diced
½ cup shredded carrots
½ avocado, diced (optional)
1 cup shredded Romaine lettuce

For the Dressing:
3 heaping tbsp. mayonnaise (lite is fine)
2 ½ tbsp. sweet teriyaki
1 tsp. spicy Dijon mustard
1 tsp. ginger powder
1 tsp. garlic powder

Warm up your pita breads in the microwave oven for 30 seconds and set aside.

In a small mixing bowl mash your tuna and then add all the apple, pear and carrots. Mix gently with a spoon. Stuff the whole wheat pitas with shredded lettuce and then add your tuna mixture and top off with sliced avocado.

For the dressing: In a small bowl add all your dressing ingredients and mix well with a fork until well combined. Pour over your tuna in pita and enjoy!

TIP

I use this dressing for a myriad of dishes. I find it works particularly well as a marinade for tilapia, salmon or tuna steak.

Falafel Turkey Lamb Burgers

SERVES 2-4

I was doing work for Manischewitz a few years ago for their annual cook-off contest, where the winner that year was for a falafel slider. I loved the concept so much that I created my own version that I make all the time for dinner at home. Thank you Amy Siegal for a great idea; hope you don't mind my extreme tweaking.

1 lb. ground turkey
1 lb. ground lamb
½ red onion, diced
½ **tsp.** fresh minced garlic
½ **cup** canned chick peas, mashed
1 package falafel mix
2 tsp. dried cilantro
2 tsp. dried mint leaves
3 tbsp. extra virgin olive oil

In a large mixing bowl add all your ingredients with the exception of the olive oil. Combine everything well and form your burgers, they should be about ¾ inch thick patties. Lay them on a non-stick griddle or on a greased cookie sheet and lightly brush the tops with the olive oil. Bake for 20 minutes and serve on burger buns or in pita bread with techina sauce.

▸ **Did you know?** Where a falafel originated is a debated question. Although some believe it originated in India, people make cases that its origin was Egypt and some people think it was originally a Hebrew food.

TIP

Recently I needed a new idea for a party appetizer. So, I made these falafel burgers into mini meatballs, wrapped each one with a slice of roasted red pepper for some color, served them on a stick with a little Techina dipping sauce and scored a huge hit.

Falafel Turkey Lamb Burgers

Lamb Pitas

SERVES 4

There are those wives who get diamonds or flowers, and there are those like me who get lamb! My darling husband has his own ideas of what would make charming gifts. Whenever Dov feels like giving me a gift, I get cases of meat or hotel size bottles of ketchup and mayonnaise. How can a girl not love such a guy? Early on in our marriage, Dov noticed that I really loved cooking and eating lamb; it must be the Moroccan in me. He came home one night and "surprised" me with a 20 lb. case of chopped lamb. As you can imagine, I had to be inventive and ended up eating many variations of these lamb pitas for lunch and dinner for the next several months.

1 small white onion, diced
1 tsp. extra virgin olive oil
1½ tsp. ground cumin
1 tsp. curry powder
½ tsp. coriander
1 tsp. dried mint
Pinch of Kosher salt
1 lb. ground lamb
½ seedless cucumber, chopped
½ cup grape tomatoes, diced
2 leaves of Romaine lettuce, roughly chopped

4 whole pitas, slightly toasted
1 cup cooked couscous or rice (optional)

In a large frying pan on medium-high heat, sauté the onions in the olive oil for about 3 minutes till they turn translucent and soft. Add all the spices to the onions and mix well with a wooden spoon. Add the chopped lamb to the onions and mix well, using the wooden spoon to break the lamb into small pea-size pieces. Cover the pan and let the lamb cook for about 6-8 minutes. Remove the lamb and place into a small mixing bowl; add to it the cucumbers and tomatoes and mix lightly.

Layer pitas the following way: First place a little chopped lettuce at the bottom of the pita followed by some couscous or rice. Lastly, top off with heaping spoonfuls of the lamb mixture. Serve hot or cold with techina or pareve cream dressing.

BONUS RECIPE ▶ Pareve Ranch Dressing

1 cup Tofutti sour cream
or yogurt
2 tbsp. fresh lemon juice
1 tsp. chopped garlic

2 tbsp. fresh dill, chopped
1 tsp. fresh mint or cilantro
Pinch of Kosher salt
Pinch of black pepper

Blend everything well in small bowl and serve.

TIP

Most local butchers will grind up lamb for you if the chopped version is not readily available; otherwise, this recipe works great with cubed lamb chops. For a more economic version, try chopped turkey or chicken for a little different but just as tasty result.

Quesadillas

SERVES 2

This is a fairly new introduction into my lunch repertoire. I was in the City one day with some girlfriends and we came across this all-vegan kosher restaurant, where the only thing on the menu that appealed to me was their quesadillas. I loved the concept of them and so ran home right away and made my own much tastier version. I usually serve them with a side of guacamole and a little sour cream and spicy salsa.

4 10-inch whole wheat corn tortilla (or any variety you like)
½ red onion, chopped
1 cup sliced Button mushrooms
1 cup chopped plum tomatoes
¼ cup sliced black olives
1 cup skim Mozzarella cheese

Preheat oven to 375 degrees.

In a frying pan that has been sprayed, add the onions, mushrooms, tomatoes and red peppers. Sauté for about 3-4 minutes, until the vegetables are soft, but still a little al dente.

Spray a cookie sheet and lay two tortillas flat down. Divide the sautéed vegetables between the two tortillas and then sprinkle the black olives and cheese. Cover each vegetable laden tortilla with the other two tortillas, making a large round sandwich. Place in oven and cook for about 8-10 minutes until cheese fully melts. Slice as you would a pizza and serve hot with guacamole, salsa verde and sour cream.

BONUS RECIPE ▶ Salsa Verde

Salsa verde is traditionally made with tomatillos, something I almost never have in my house, so I use regular tomatoes. My salsa is not always as green as it should be, but it's just as tasty.

4 large tomatoes, sliced in half   *¼ tsp. sugar*
½ cup chopped white onions   *½ jalapeno pepper, stemmed,*
½ cup cilantro leaves   *seeded & chopped (optional)*
1 tbsp. fresh lime juice   *1 tsp. Kosher salt*

Blend everything well in small bowl and serve.

▶ **Did you know?** Quesadilla is a Mexican food made primarily of cheese inside a folded corn or wheat tortilla and cooked until the cheese melts. Occasionally, a second ingredient is added with the cheese to add variety to the dish. The word comes from Spanish, and literally means "cheesy tortilla".

This is a great, healthy, low-fat lunch or dinner that you and your kids will love. It is very filling and extremely easy for them to make themselves. Change the ingredients and have many variations of these delicious quesadillas.

Basic Desserts

Sara G.'s Famous Vanilla Cheese Cake

A few years ago at one of my book signings in Cedarhurst, NY I met someone who had the tenacity to ask if she could work for me. "I'll do anything" was Sara G.'s way into my store and into my heart. She is an exceptional baker who makes the most awesome cheesecakes, that we can barely keep in stock, and she has become my right hand man. Every Monday night, I make her gourmet dinners to make sure she doesn't ever leave me.

For the Crust:
2 cups graham crackers
1 stick butter

For the Cake:
1 lb. cream cheese
3 eggs
1 cup sugar
1 pint sour cream
1 tsp. lemon zest
1 tsp. vanilla extract

Preheat oven to 350 degrees. Spray the bottom of a 9-inch spring-form pan. Wrap outside of the spring-form with aluminum foil.

With a food processor, pulse graham crackers until they are fine. Then, melt the butter and mix butter into ground graham crackers. Press firmly into bottom of spring-form and refrigerate.

Place cream cheese into electric mixer fitted with the flat beater. Mix cream cheese until smooth and no lumps are present. Add eggs one at a time, scraping down sides of bowl intermittently. Add sugar. Add sour cream until well combined. Add lemon zest and vanilla.

Pour batter into spring-form. Place inside large full steam pan and then fill pan 2/3 of the way up with water. Bake for 1 hour or until the cheesecake has set, but still has a little wiggle in the middle. Refrigerate until cool before serving.

BONUS RECIPE ▶ Chocolate Ganache Glaze

Basic ganache consists of just two ingredients: semi-sweet chocolate and heavy cream. The meaning of the French word "ganache" is "cushion," as the cream seems to "cushion" both the flavor and texture of chocolate.

2 cups heavy whipping cream
1 ¼ lbs. bittersweet chocolate, roughly chopped into small pieces

Bring the cream to a boil, and then remove from the heat immediately. Right away, pour the hot cream over the bowl of chopped chocolate.

Let it stand, covered, for a moment to soften the chocolate, then whisk until smooth. For best results, let it cool at room temperature, and then pour onto your cheesecake.

TIP

I use this vanilla cheesecake for the base of most of my cheesecakes. Be creative and add chocolate chips or chunks of cookie dough for some new variations.

Great Aunt Titi's Biscotti

My great aunt Titi makes the most wonderful almond bars. My aunt's are always perfectly thin small biscotti bars, and you just can't stop eating once you start. I begged her for her recipe and she was happy to oblige. However, I usually add chocolate chips and make them the traditional biscotti size.

2 eggs
¾ cup sugar
½ cup oil
1 tsp. almond extract
Pinch cinnamon
2 cups flour
1 ¼ tsp. baking powder
½ cup sliced almonds, toasted

Preheat oven to 350 degrees.

Mix first 5 ingredients together in a large mixing bowl. Switch to your paddle attachment and then slowly add the flour and baking powder. Mix just to combine for about 1-2 minutes. Remove bowl from mixer and gently fold in the toasted sliced almonds.

Divide dough in half. Shape each half into a 9"x 2" log. Place logs crosswise, 4 inches apart, on large cookie sheet. With pastry brush, brush tops and sides of logs with egg. Bake logs 25 minutes. Cool logs on cookie sheet on wire rack 10 minutes.

Place 1 log on cutting board. With serrated knife, cut warm log crosswise into ½-inch-thick diagonal slices. Place slices upright, ¼ inch apart, on cookie sheets. Repeat with remaining log. Bake slices 15 minutes to allow biscotti to dry out. Cool completely on sheets on wire racks. (Biscotti will harden as they cool.) Store biscotti in tightly covered container.

Dark Chocolate Cupcakes

MAKES 12

Cupcakes have become all the rage lately and I have joined that band wagon many years ago. That first bite of a well-made cupcake with extra frosting is what dreams are made of. Rivky E. and I once went to a cupcake baking class in the city, where we thought we would learn secrets untold. However, after a whole day wasted and that not being the case, there was one thing we did learn; we both love cupcakes way too much.

1 stick unsalted butter, cut into 4 pieces
2 oz. bittersweet chocolate, chopped
½ cup Dutch-processed cocoa powder
¾ cup all purpose flour
½ tsp. baking soda
¾ tsp. baking powder
2 large eggs, whisked
¾ cup sugar
1 tsp. vanilla extract
½ tsp. salt
½ cup sour cream

Preheat oven to 350 degrees.

Combine butter, chocolate, and cocoa in heat-proof pan. Set bowl over saucepan containing lightly simmering water; heat mixture until butter and chocolate are melted and then whisk until smooth and fully combined. Set aside to cool.

Whisk flour, baking soda and baking powder to combine. Add the whisked eggs and combine; add sugar, vanilla and salt and whisk until fully incorporated. Add cooled chocolate mixture and whisk until combined; whisk sour cream until combined. The batter should be thick.

Divide batter evenly among lined muffin pan cups. Bake for 18-20 minutes. Cool on wire rack before frosting.

BONUS RECIPE ▶ **Buttercream**

1 ¼ sticks unsalted butter, softened to room temperature
1 tsp. vanilla extract

1 ¼ cup confectioners sugar
Pinch of salt
1 tbsp. heavy cream

In a mixer with whisk attachment, beat butter at med-high speed until smooth, about 20 seconds. Add the confectioners sugar and salt; beat at medium-low speed for 45 seconds. Scrape down bowl and beat at medium speed for another 15 seconds: scrape bowl and add the vanilla and heavy cream, and beat at medium speed for another 10 seconds or until everything is incorporated, then increase speed to medium high and beat until light and fluffy, about 4 minutes.

For Chocolate Buttercream: Use the above recipe; just reduce the confectioners sugar to one cup and then after you beat in the heavy cream add 4 ounces of cooled melted chocolate.

 TIP When making cupcakes, instead of doubling the recipe when you need more than 12, it is preferable to make 2 separate batches.

Dark Chocolate Cupcakes

Grilled Grapefruit Cobbler

MAKES 4

The first time I saw this grapefruit dessert I was floored. Broiled grapefruit! But the spicy tangy topping with the sweet grapefruit is outta this world.

2 large red grapefruits, halved crosswise and sectioned
3 tbsp. dark brown sugar
1 ½ tsp. flour
¼ tsp. ground ginger
⅛ tsp. ground cinnamon
2 tbsp. unsalted butter, room temperature

In a small bowl combine the sugar, flour, ginger, cinnamon and butter and blend well. Portion the mixture evenly between the mixture halves, smearing it on the top of each one. Place in oven that has been set to broil and broil until top is golden brown and bubbly, about 5 minutes. Serve immediately.

TIP
This makes a great party dessert. Prep the grapefruits in advance and put it into the broiler 10 minutes before you are ready to serve. Simple & delicious.

Zucchini Muffins
(the diet version)
MAKES 12 JUMBO MUFFINS OR 24 REGULAR SIZE MUFFINS

I put the original zucchini muffin recipe in my first cookbook The Dairy Gourmet *without realizing that I was disappointing many of my loyal fans and customers who really wanted my diet version of this recipe. So for all of you who have called, emailed, texted and come into the store to protest, here is my not-so-secret-anymore zucchini muffin recipe. Enjoy!*

2 extra large eggs
¼ cup sugar
¾ cup baking Splenda
¼ cup oil
1 ½ cups applesauce
3 cups flour
1 tsp. cinnamon
1 ½ tsp. baking powder
1 tsp. Kosher salt
½ tsp. baking soda
2 medium zucchinis, skin on & shredded

Preheat oven to 375 degrees.

In a large mixing bowl on medium speed, mix the eggs, sugar, Splenda, oil, and applesauce together. Switch to a paddle attachment and let the mixer run on low for a few minutes. In a separate bowl sift together the flour, cinnamon, baking powder, salt, and baking soda. Slowly add these dry ingredients to the wet ingredients in the mixer and combine them well. Add the shredded zucchini to the batter and mix for another minute till the zucchini is fully combined.

Spray your muffin tins well with non-stick spray and fill them with the zucchini batter about ¾ way full. Bake for about 25-30 minutes or until toothpick comes out clean. Serve them warm or cold.

Red Velvet Cake

MAKES 1 CAKE OR 18 CUPCAKES

A few Purims ago, I was newly married and felt I had to put a little bit more effort than I normally do into that year's shaloch manos. I mean, they are not just from me alone anymore; they have to be a little better than my usual wine and chocolates. I decided, what are easier and cheaper than cupcakes? Red velvet cupcakes particularly; they're colorful, very festive looking, unbelievably delicious, and not many people make them. I went through about 4 different recipes before I perfected this one, went to T.J. Maxx and found some very cool, funky-looking black and white plates to put the red velvets on, and the Leizerowskis had a memorable Purim gift our very first year that has now become tradition every Purim since.

NOTE: The exact origin of red velvet cake is not known. A 1972 cookbook, *James Beard's American Cookery*, tells that the additions of acidic ingredients like buttermilk and vinegar react chemically with cocoa to produce a reddish shade. Though Beard's recipes use food coloring, cocoa used to be less alkaline than it is now, so it is possible that cooks began adding red food coloring to mimic the effect of acidic ingredients on older types of cocoa. Another popular notion is that while foods were rationed during World War II, bakers used boiled beets to enhance the color of their cakes. Boiled grated beets or beet baby food are found in some red velvet cake recipes, where they also serve to retain moisture.

- 2 ½ **cups** flour
- 1 ½ **cups** sugar
- 1 **tsp.** baking soda
- 1 **tsp.** salt
- 1 **tsp.** Dutch cocoa powder
- 1 ½ **cups** vegetable oil
- 1 **cup** heavy cream + 2 **tsp.** lemon juice (combine them first and let sit till ready to add to dry ingredients)
- 2 large eggs

- 2 **tbsp.** red food coloring
- 1 **tsp.** white distilled vinegar
- 1 **tsp.** pure vanilla extract

Cream Cheese Frosting:

- 1 **lb.** cream cheese, softened
- 2 sticks unsalted butter
- 1 **tsp.** pure vanilla extract
- 4 **cups** confectioners sugar, sifted

Preheat the oven to 350 degrees.

Sift together the flour, sugar, baking soda, salt, and cocoa powder and set aside. In a large mixing bowl gently beat together the oil, heavy cream, eggs, food coloring, vinegar, and vanilla. Slowly add the sifted dry ingredients to the wet and mix until creamy smooth and thoroughly combined.

Line cupcake tins with cupcake holders and spray with non-stick spray. Divide the batter evenly among cupcake tins 2/3 full. Bake in oven for about 10 minutes, then rotate cupcakes in oven and bake for another 10 minutes. Remove from oven and cool completely before frosting.

For the Cream Cheese Frosting: In a large mixing bowl, beat the cream cheese, butter and vanilla together until smooth. Add the sugar and on low speed, beat until incorporated. Increase the speed to high and mix until very light and fluffy. Using the back of a flat knife spread the cream cheese frosting on top of the cooled red velvet cupcake and serve. You can also garnish with shaved chocolate.

Smoothies

Strawberry Blueberry Smoothie
MAKES 2

½ **cup** frozen blueberries
½ **cup** frozen strawberries
2 tbsp. honey
1½ **cup** Skim milk
Pinch ground ginger (optional)
Fresh whipped cream

Combine the two fruits, honey and milk in blender and blend till smooth. Sprinkle the cup with fresh ginger, pour the smoothie and top with fresh whipped cream and blueberries.

NOTE: You can use 1 ½ cups of ice with fresh blueberries and strawberries for the same results.

Orange Strawberry Smoothie
MAKES 2

The tofu in this drink makes a great source of daily protein and the creamy texture is a great substitute for milk.

1 ½ **cups** frozen strawberries (about 16 pieces)
½ **lb.** silken tofu
⅔ **cup** orange juice
¼ **cup** honey
1 tsp. pure vanilla extract

Combine all ingredients in blender and blend till smooth.

Butter Cookies

MAKES ABOUT 3 DOZEN

I searched for a very long time for the perfect butter cookie like the ones that Peppridge Farms makes. This is the recipe. I make these all the time and use them with different combinations of toppings and fillings for the store. But nothing is as decadent as a bite of these butter cookies and a tall cup of cappuccino with extra whip.

3 sticks butter
1 cup sugar
1 tsp. vanilla extract
3 ½ cups all-purpose flour
¼ tsp. salt

Preheat oven 350 degrees.

Sift together flour and salt, set aside. In a bowl of an electric mixer fitted with the paddle attachment, mix together butter and sugar until combined. Add vanilla. Add flour mixture to butter batter. Mix on low speed until dough starts to come together. Place dough onto a lightly floured surface, form into a flat disk, wrap in plastic and place in refrigerator for 30 minutes.

On a flour dusted surface roll dough ¼-inch thick and cut into round shapes. Bake 20-25 minutes.

Smore Cookies

Here is one of the many ways I use the Butter Cookie recipe, found on the previous page. These Smore Cookies are great as a kid's dessert or sophisticated party cookie.

For the Cookie:
For cookie recipe, see Butter Cookies on page 188.

For the Smores:
1 cup melted bittersweet chocolate
1 cup creamy peanut butter
1 jar marshmallow fluff
Ground nuts

STEP 1:
Dip all your cookies into the melted bittersweet chocolate. Set in refrigerator for ten minutes.

STEP 2:
Spread peanut butter on one half.

STEP 3:
Spread marshmallow fluff over peanut butter.

STEP 4:
Top with a second chocolate-coated cookie. Garnish with ground nuts.

TIP If serving at a party, best to freeze these cookies and serve semi frozen, to avoid a chocolate-y mess.

Decadence

MAKES 2

This is a drink that we created in Tastebuds that just makes me salivate. It truly lives up to its name. It makes a great dessert at the end of a great dairy meal.

2 favorite brand chocolate chip cookies
2 scoops chocolate ice cream
1 tsp. amaretto flavoring
2 tsp. mini chocolate chips
1 tbsp. chocolate syrup
¼ cup milk

Blend one cookie in a blender, and add the rest of the ingredients. Blend until smooth. Serve in large glass topped with fresh whipped cream and the extra cookie.

BONUS RECIPE ▸ **Peanut Butter Shake**

2 scoops vanilla ice cream
1 tbsp. creamy peanut butter
1 tbsp. chopped nuts
2 tsp. mini chocolate chips
1 tbsp. chocolate syrup
¼ cup milk

Blend all ingredients in a blender till smooth. Top off with whipped cream, and garnish with more chocolate chips and chopped nuts.

BONUS RECIPE ▸ **Rocky Road Shake**

1 scoop vanilla ice cream
1 scoop chocolate ice cream
1 tbsp. peanut butter
2 tsp. whole peanuts
2 tsp. chocolate chips
1 tsp. chocolate syrup
¼ cup milk
5-6 mini marshmallows

Blend all ingredients in a blender, except the marshmallows, until smooth. Add the marshmallow to the bottom of a large cup and pour in the blended shake. Top with whipped cream and extra nuts.

Blondies

There is nothing like a great chocolate brownie that you can dip in milk for an afternoon snack. Well, I must say, these Blondies are a real close second best, and are just as decadent as any chocolate brownie I have ever tasted. Lately I have been adding crushed-up bits of Oreo cookies and mini marshmallows along with half of the chips and nuts, where the results can only be described in one word, YUMMY!

2 cups all-purpose flour
¾ tsp. baking powder
½ tsp. baking soda
½ tsp. salt
2 sticks butter, room temperature
1 ½ cups light brown sugar
½ cup sugar
2 large eggs
1 tsp. vanilla extract
1 cup chocolate chips
1 cup chopped walnuts
1 cup shredded coconut

Preheat oven to 325 degrees. Spray a 9x13 baking pan.

Whisk together the flour, baking powder, baking soda and salt.

In a bowl of an electric mixer fitted with the paddle attachment beat the butter until creamy and smooth. Add both sugars, and beat until well incorporated. Add eggs one at a time, then vanilla. On low speed add dry ingredients just until well incorporated (do not over mix). Using a rubber spatula, lightly mix in chips, nuts, and coconut. Pour into pan and even out the top with the spatula.

Bake 40 minutes or until toothpick comes out clean. Cool for 15 minutes before cutting.

Diet Muffins

MAKES 12 MUFFINS

When I first started Tastebuds, I took the Weight Watcher 3 point recipe for their basic muffin and started to make them for the store in all varieties. They have become extremely popular, to the point where I have people ordering them by the dozens on a weekly basis. I asked one customer who orders them sometimes twice a week, "Where do these muffins go?" Her reply: "My husband, cleaning lady, and I have one every day for breakfast and one for a treat during the day."

1 cup flour
1 tsp. baking powder
½ tsp. salt
1 large egg
1 large egg white

½ cup plus **2 tbsp.** packed light brown sugar
¼ cup applesauce
3 tsp. canola oil
1 tsp. vanilla extract
6 tbsp. semi sweet chocolate chips or
1 ½ cups blueberries

Preheat oven to 400 degrees.

Coat a 12-hole muffin tin with cooking spray. Sift together flour, baking powder and salt in a medium bowl. Set aside.

Separate the 2 eggs, placing both whites in a medium bowl and saving only one yolk in a large mixing bowl. Set whites aside. Add brown sugar, applesauce, oil and vanilla to yolk in the large bowl. Mix on medium speed until well blended. Lower mixer speed and slowly add flour mixture slowly and stir until well combined. Remove bowl from mixer and set aside.

In another mixer bowl, beat egg whites on high until soft peaks form. Using a rubber spatula, gently fold the whites into the muffin batter. Then add the chocolate chips or blueberries into the batter. Mix just to combine (don't over-mix).

Scoop out batter using a medium size ice cream scooper, one scoop per muffin liner. Bake in pre-heated oven for about 20-25 minutes or until toothpick comes out clean.

BONUS RECIPE ▶ ## Sarah's Diet Chocolate Chip Muffin

If I am going to have a "diet" muffin I prefer the ones that are low in sugar and have regular full fat. The texture and taste of the muffin satisfies my craving more than the spongier, drier, low-fat, low-sugar muffins that I come across. So here is my version of a sugar-free, regular fat, delicious chocolate chip muffin.

1 ½ cups flour
½ cup baking Splenda
2 ¼ tsp. baking powder
½ tsp. baking soda
½ tsp. Kosher salt

1 cup buttermilk or (1 cup heavy cream + ½ tbsp. lemon juice)
2 large eggs
½ cup semi-sweet chocolate chips

Sift all the dry ingredients in one bowl (minus the chocolate chips) and mix all the wet ingredients in a second bowl. Slowly add the dry ingredients to the wet ingredients and then slowly fold in the chocolate chips. Scoop batter into lined muffin tins and bake in preheated 400 degree oven for 15-20 minutes.

Granola Bars

Most granola bars are simply candy bars in disguise, with very little fiber, lots of processed carbs, and a ton of sugar. You're better off making your own healthier version.

I make homemade granola all the time at Tastebuds and at home. It's a great snack and one batch lasts quite a long time in the freezer. One day as I was looking through one of my many cooking magazines, I came across a recipe for homemade granola bars. That recipe called for karo syrup and peanut butter, but it gave me great inspiration to tweak my homemade granola recipe to create these delicious bars.

2 cups old fashion oats
½ cup sliced almonds
½ cup chopped pecans
1 cup shredded coconut
3 tbsp. butter
⅔ cup honey
¼ cup light brown sugar
1 ½ tsp. vanilla extract
¼ tsp. Kosher salt
¼ cup chopped pitted dates
½ cup dried figs
¼ cup chopped dried apricots
¼ cup crasins
¼ cup raisins

Preheat oven to 350 degrees. Spray a 9x13 pan and line with parchment paper.

Mix oats, almonds, pecans and coconut together and bake on a sheet pan 10-12 minutes, occasionally stirring, until light brown in color. Transfer to large mixing bowl. Reduce oven temperature to 300 degrees.

Place butter, honey, brown sugar, vanilla, and salt in a sauce pan over medium heat and bring to a boil. Cook for one minute, occasionally stirring and then pour over oatmeal mixture. Add dry fruit and mix well.

Pour mixture into prepared pan, pressing evenly. Bake for 25-30 minutes, or until golden brown. Cool 2-3 hours before cutting. Serve at room temperature.